Jeremiah Williams Cummings, Domenico Speranza

Songs for Catholic schools and aids to memory for the catechism

Jeremiah Williams Cummings, Domenico Speranza

Songs for Catholic schools and aids to memory for the catechism

ISBN/EAN: 9783742822598

Manufactured in Europe, USA, Canada, Australia, Japa

Cover: Foto ©Andreas Hilbeck / pixelio.de

Manufactured and distributed by brebook publishing software
(www.brebook.com)

Jeremiah Williams Cummings, Domenico Speranza

Songs for Catholic schools and aids to memory for the catechism

PREFACE.

I RESPECTFULLY ask of the Catholic public a fair trial for this collection of melodies, prepared at the urgent request of Bishops and Clergymen in every part of the United States. It bears the title of "Songs for Catholic Schools," being chiefly designed for singing or recitation in Sunday-schools and day-schools under Catholic direction, but it will be found useful also by church choirs, religious communities, and private families. It is the first original collection of the kind ever published in this country. This fact, it is hoped, will excuse its imperfections, and at the same time obtain for it a friendly reception on the part of all who have at heart the religious improvement of American Catholic children.

The "Definitions and Aids to Memory," in the second part of the book, are a brief catechism in rhyme, a plan of conveying religious instruction which has been tried with excellent results among young and illiterate persons in other countries. The singing or chanting of such rhymes causes them to be learned quicker, and impresses them more deeply on the memory. We have, therefore, set to music the portions best adapted for the purpose.

The getting up of such a work involves a vast amount of labor, care, and expense; that it may go forth with God's blessing and do some good, is the earnest prayer of its author.

J. W. CUMMINGS.

St. Stephen's Church, New York.

SONGS FOR CATHOLIC SCHOOLS.

TO ST. STEPHEN.

HOLY Stephen, Chief of Martyrs,
    Thee we hail with special love—
Mary chose thee for our patron
    'Mid all saints of heaven above:
Hear the voices of thy children,
    Kneeling fondly at thy shrine;
Fill our hearts with love for Jesus,
    With a fervent love like thine.

Fond Protector, we have loved thee
    For thy faith so bold and true;
'Twas that faith whose simple wisdom
    Overcame both Greek and Jew.
Teach us, like thee, on our foreheads
    To impress the sacred sign,
And to meet our faith's opponents
    With a courage like to thine.

1*

Strong with rage, the heartless tyrants
　　Dragged thee to the City gate—
Stones were hurled in fearful volleys—
　　Holy youth, they've sealed thy fate!
With the odor of the victim,
　　Earliest slain for Jesus' faith,
Rose a prayer imploring pardon
　　For the men who gave it death.

Stephen for his persecutors
　　Prays as Christ had prayed before;
And th' Apostle of the nations
　　To the cause of truth comes o'er.
Proto-martyr, teach thy children
　　Good for evil to return;
Teach the hearts of unbelievers
　　With a love like Paul's to burn.

Life in doing good thou spendest,
　　And when dying dost behold
Thy sweet Master clad in glory,
　　Mortal tongue hath never told.
Make us imitate thy virtues,
　　Blessed Saint—we are thine own,
And unite us all in heaven
　　Near the footstool of thy throne.

THE MUSIC OF NATURE.

THERE's music in the bubbling rill
   That frolics o'er the mead,
That makes the silver daisy bloom,
   And laves the nodding reed.
There's music in the gentle breeze
   That whispers through the wood,
And softly sings, to mortal things,
   The praise of Nature's God.

There's music in the shower that falls
   Upon a sultry day,
To spread new verdure o'er the fields,
   And cheer the drooping spray.
There's music in the frisky lamb
   That loves the verdant sod,
And sporting sings, to mortal things,
   The praise of Nature's God.

There's music in the tiny throats
   That hail the rising sun,
That cheer the traveler's weary way,
   Across the woodland dun.
There's music in the busy bee
   That makes the flow'ret nod,
And humming sings, to mortal things,
   The praise of Nature's God.

There's music in the bright cascade
  That dashes from the steep,
Along the banks where rivers roll
  Their waters to the deep,
And, driven by the tempest's breatl
  O'er foaming ocean's flood,
The billow sings, to mortal things,
  The praise of Nature's God.

Thus toward the skies an endless hymn
  Of earthly notes ascends,
And with the music of the spheres
  In daily concert blends.
One voice is harsh, one voice alone
  Through all the world's abode—
The sinner sings in praise of things
  Forbidden by his God.

THE MESSENGER ANGEL.

THE Messenger Angel descending at night,
Chased silence and shadow with music and
  light.

The shepherds of Bethlehem heard on the
    plain
The Messenger Angel, and this was his strain:
"May peace be to mortals and glory to Hea-
    ven—
The Promised of old to mankind has been
    given;
Rejoice at the splendors that herald his birth,
The Saviour, the Saviour has come upon earth.

"The fields are adorned with the verdure of
    May,
And winter's chill bosom with roses is gay;
The winds that made war on the face of the
    deep,
Have sought their dark caverns and lain down
    to sleep.
'Mid nature's glad triumph rise, mortals, arise,
The mystery viewing with holy surprise;
Rejoice at the glory that heralds his birth,
The Saviour, the Saviour has come upon earth.

"The wise men of nations advance from afar,
Led on by the shining of Jacob's bright star;
To Bethlehem's grotto their treasures they
    bring,
And kneel at the shrine of the heavenly King.

The Gentiles in darkness are slumb'ring no
    more,
But worship the God whom they knew not
    before,
And follow the light which announces his
    birth—
The Saviour, the Saviour has come upon
    earth."

Yet chanted the Seraph, when rapturous strains
From thousands of angels awakened the plains;
Ethereal splendor encircled the throng
That caught up his theme and re-echoed his
    song.
The burden was swelled by each heavenly
    voice:
"The Expected is come: happy mortals re-
    joice!
Rejoice at the glories that herald his birth—
The Saviour, the Saviour has come upon
    earth."

MORNING PRAYER.

THE earth, O Lord, rejoices,
 And sings with glad acclaim,
A hymn of many voices,
 In honor of thy name.
We join the happy chorus,
 That hails the morning light;
And bless the Lord that o'er us,
 Kept loving watch all night.

Our every thought and action,
 We offer up to thee;
From folly and distraction,
 We beg thee keep us free.
Let no profane example,
 No censure, no applause,
Lead us this day to trample,
 O Lord, upon thy laws.

It pleased thee, Lord, to make us,
 That we might serve thee here;
Let not thy grace forsake us,
 But keep us in thy fear.
Preserve our life, O Father,
 That we may serve thee still;
But let us lose it rather
 Than disobey thy will.

HAIL! VIRGIN OF VIRGINS

HAIL! Virgin of virgins!
   Thy praises we sing,
Thy throne is in heaven,
   Thy Son is its King.
The Saints and the Angels
   Thy glory proclaim;
All nations devoutly
   Bow down at thy name.

Let all sing of Mary,
   The mystical Rod,
The Mirror of Justice,
   The Handmaid of God.
Let valley and mountain
   Unite in her praise;
The sea with its waters,
   The sun with its rays.

Let souls that are holy
   Still holier be,
To sing with the angels
   Sweet Mary, of thee
Let all who are sinners
   To virtue return,
That hearts without number
   With thy love may burn.

Thy name is our power,
  Thy love is our light;
We praise thee at morning,
  At noon and at night.
We thank thee, we bless thee,
  When happy and free;
When, tempted by Satan,
  We call upon thee.

The world does not love thee,
  Oh beautiful one!
Because it despises
  The cross of thy Son.
But thou art the Mother
  Of all Adam's race;
The birth-stain of Eva
  'Tis thine to efface.

Oh! be then our Mother,
  And pray to the Lord,
That all may acknowledge
  And worship His Word;
That good men with courage
  May walk in His ways,
And bad men converted
  May join in His praise.
2

THE INVOCATION.

GOD of glory,
  God of might,
Foe of error,
  Friend of right,—
Roll the tempest
  Far away,
Smile in sunbeams
  As we pray.

We are prostrate
  At thy throne,
Knowing, fearing
  Thee alone.
Thou art Master
  Of us all,—
Nations by Thee
  Stand or fall.

Who can conquer
  Thee, O, Lord?
What is stronger
  Than Thy word?
What Thou blessest
  Must prevail;
What Thou cursest
  Can but fail.

At thy bidding,
.Like a scroll,
Heaven its blue arch
Did unroll.
Stars and planets
Sprung to light,
From the bosom
Of the night.

'Tis thy wisdom
Guides the sun,
Till his daily
Race is run ;
And when evening
Spreads its haze,
Silver moonbeams
Speak Thy praise.

O'er the waters,
At thy word,
Earth upheaving
Owned its Lord.
Yearly traveling,
Space immense,
Earth still blesses
Providence.

To thine image
    Man was made,
And in Eden's
    Sunny glade,
Blest with graces
    Bright and strong,
Good to follow,
    Shunning wrong.

Led by Satan
    To rebel,
From thy favor
    Soon he fell.
But as Adam
    Stood, we stand,
Raised by Jesus'
    Outstretched hand.

God of Mercy,
    Truth and Right,
Give Thy ransomed
    Children light,
Here His sacred
    Law to prize,
And to see Him
    In the skies.

THE CHURCH.

WORLD of Grace! mysterious Temple!
  Holy, Apostolic, One!
Never changing, ever blessing
  Ev'ry age and ev'ry zone;
Church, sweet mother! may all nations
  Know thee, love thee as before,
May thy children learn to prize thee,
  Daily, hourly, more and more.

Where on earth the hapless region
  Not illumined by her light?
Where the shore her saintly heralds
  Never gladdened with their sight?
Unconfined by wave or mountain,
  Spreads her voice from pole to pole,
Threat'ning Hell or pledging Heaven
  To the pure or guilty soul.

Vainly did the haughty Roman
  Smite her cheek with power's rod,
Vainly did the subtler Attic
  Spread his toils where'er she trod.
Through the adverse crowd she wended,
  In the triumph of her might,
Baffling Warrior, Sage, and Sophist,
  Skilled in wiles or bold in fight.

2*

From his couch of fragrant roses
   She has torn the Sybarite,
She has checked the rushing Vandal
   In the hottest of the fight;
She has tracked the Northern Savage
   Even to his rocky den;
She has tamed the vengeful Huron
   Wandering in the woody glen.

She has written in the tablets
   Of the infantine Chinese;
She has sung amid the bowers
   Of the happy Bengalese;
She has snatched the trembling Hindoo
   From the smoking funeral pile;
She has lit the dusky features
   Of the bond-slave with a smile.

All of Truth, and naught of Error,
   Is her dowry—hers alone;
While her life of inward beauty
   Knows—hopes—loves the Triune One.
From the heart of her Beloved
   Flows a fount in seven-fold stream,
Whence her children draw the waters
   Lit by Heaven's quickening beam.

Church of God! mysterious Temple!
　Holy, Apostolic, One!
Never changing, ever blessing
　Ev'ry age and ev'ry zone.
Church, sweet mother! may all nations
　Know thee, love thee as before,
May thy children learn to prize thee,
　Daily, hourly, more and more.

THE ASCENSION.

Rejoice, oh ye children of bondage!
　The night of your grief has gone by,
And bright as the sun is at morning,
　Your Lord has ascended on high.
Lift up the bright portals of glory,
　Blest Angels, to let in your King,
And hasten the hymn of His triumph,
　On golden harps bravely to sing.

He bowed Him in death, as a victim,
　To atone for the crime of the world;
Sin's sceptre from Sin He hath wrested,
　Death's dart against Death He hath hurled.
Great Father, the shafts of Thy anger
　Now happily idle will be—
Thou smilest in peace on Thy creatures,
　No longer rebellious to Thee.

Oh Saints, that in glory refulgent,
  Burst forth from the tombs where you lay,
And back o'er a path yet untrodden,
  Come out with your Chief into day:
How looked He, how seemed He, the victor
  From worlds He had conquered below,
To worlds far above the last planet,
  Prepared as their Monarch to go?

Oh, none but your tongue, or a Seraph's,
  May tell of the Infinite One,
Whom kings in their glory resemble,
  As glow-worms resemble the sun.
Yet we can exult in your triumph,
  Ye servants and friends of the Lord—
We hope, humbly hope yet to share it,
  Through grace of the all-saving Word.

This day, in the heart of poor mortals
  Reign gladness and peace.—It is well!
This day the chill shadow of sadness
  Should darken no dwelling but Hell.
This day, let the prayers of the youthful,
  Like incense, to Heaven ascend,
And gain for the souls of the ransomed
  The grace to love God to the end.

THE BLESSING.

CHILDREN of St. Stephen! raise
High the grateful notes of praise;
With the voice the heart should swell,
While the orison you tell:
    Nos cum prole pia,
    Benedicat Virgo Maria!

Jesus, God's Incarnate Word!
Mary, mother of our Lord!
Bless us, while our choral song,
Peals the sacred walls along:
    Nos cum prole pia,
    Benedicat Virgo Maria!

Bless our Church, the common home,
Where the faithful daily come,—
Now to breathe the thankful prayer,
Now to pour their sorrows there!
    Nos cum prole pia,
    Benedicat Virgo Maria!

Bless our priest who at God's shrine,
Offers up the Host Divine,—
Or His justice to adore,
Or His mercy to implore!
    Nos cum prole pia,
    Benedicat Virgo Maria!

Bless our parents, teach them still
All their duties to fulfill;
Still aright our steps to lead,
By their word, and by their deed.
      Nos cum prole pia,
      Benedicat Virgo Maria.

Bless us when in school we learn,
When we play, or home return,—
And when fails this mortal breath,
Hear us praying at our death.
      Nos cum prole pià,
      Benedicat Virgo Maria.

PRAYER AGAINST TEMPTATION.

[Arranged for the French hymn " *Puissante Protectrice.*"]

Oh, Mary! Mother Mary!
  We place our trust in thee—
Our faith shall never vary,
  Though weak the flesh may be.
Too oft with steps unwary,
  From duty's path we've bent:
Oh, Mary! Mother Mary!
  Thou teach us to repent.

The grisly form of terror
  Now rises on our way;
Now more seductive error
  Would lead our feet astray.
Satan is strong and wary,
  But thou wilt crush his might:
Oh, Mary! Mother Mary!
  Strengthen us in the fight.

From dangerous occasions
  That blind, imprudent eyes—
From treacherous persuasions
  That point not to the skies—
From mirth too light and airy,
  From thought too sad and deep:
Oh, Mary! Mother Mary!
  Thy little children keep.

Let us remember ever
  The presence of the Lord;
To serve him let's endeavor,
  In thought, in deed, in word.
As Monster, or as Fairy,
  Satan may take the field—
But Mary! Mother Mary!
  Thy name will be our shield.

HOLY COMMUNION.

AIR—AGATHE.

WHEN our Saviour wished to prove
All the fullness of his love,
He gave us ere life was spent
The thrice Holy Sacrament.
It is here his burning heart
Would to all its flames impart;
Thus He speaks with love divine,
Give me, oh give me that heart of thine.

When the dark and stormy night
Fills the soul with wild affright;
From the cloudlet where he hides
Soon a ray of comfort glides.
Where the tear of mis'ry falls,
Where the voice of sorrow calls;
Still He speaks with love divine,
Give me, oh give me that heart of thine

Can the Saint's ecstatic flight—
Can the wingèd Seraph's might,
To their Lord approach more near
Than do we poor sinners here?
God Himself we here receive,
Nobler gift He cannot give;
Yet He breathes with love divine,
Give me, oh give me that heart of thine.

THE ANNUNCIATION.

In highest heaven where stands the throne
  Of Majesty supernal,
The Archangel Gabriel came alone,
  And bowed before the Eternal.
His Lord's behests received he there,
  And toward the crystal portals
He winged his way, a herald fair
  Of peace to sinful mortals.

Each heavenly choir sang hymns of thanks
  As he to each drew nearer;
And honored all adown their ranks,
  Of God's commands the bearer.
As from the gates of pearl afar
  The princely spirit wended,
Burned every conscious sun and star
  With rays more pure and splendid.

Athwart the azure firmament
  And atmospheric ocean,
He like a dazzling meteor went
  With swift but steady motion.
He reached the earth: nor shades of night
  Nor wintry snows dare meet him,
And lilies white and roses bright,
  Burst blooming forth to greet him.

3.

He seeketh not the gilded dome
  Where reign earth's favored minions,
But in a simple Jewish home
  He rests his snowy pinions.
A lowly maiden there beholds
  The ambassador of heaven;
To her his message he unfolds—
  To her the crown is given.

Heaven's minister is heard no more
  God's wondrous works foretelling,
For he hath flown his errand o'er,
  Back to his master's dwelling.
But God fulfills the promise now,
  His Son is made our brother,
And, Mary, Queen of Virgins, thou,
  Thou art the Saviour's Mother.

THE SLEEP OF THE INFANT JESUS.

SLUMBER, haste! on dewy pinions
  From thy starry throne descend,
Gently toward yon little manger,
  Let thy golden wand extend.

On his mother's bosom slowly
  Lo! the Babe reclines his head;
Sweetly o'er his wearied senses
  Balmy sleep its charm hath spread.

Hark! the angry blast of winter
  Dies along the snowy plain;
Fainter grow the rippling murmurs
  Of Judea's distant main.
Through the pine-grove Cedron calmly
  Pours its waves adown the steep;
Silence reigns o'er things created
  While their Maker's wrapt in sleep.

But alas! a fitful shadow
  Passes o'er his features now,
Heavenly Babe, what thoughts of sorrow
  Overcast thy comely brow?
Tell, oh! tell, thou gentle mother,
  What disturbs thine Infant's rest;
Knowest thou what sad reflection
  Lurketh in his heaving breast?

Can it be this lonely grotto
  Opening on the snowy plain;
Can it be that rugged pallet
  Gives the trembling infant pain?

No! responsive to his calling
   Gilded domes would rise from earth:
But he chose a nameless dwelling
   For his poor and humble birth.

'Tis his heart that slumbers never
   Though he close his wearied eyes;
Still before his mystic vision
   Future days of strife arise.
Now he feels disgraceful fetters
   Round his weary limbs entwined;
Now the scenes of shame and torture
   Pass before his watchful mind.

Yet 'tis not the gloomy dungeon,
   Thorny scourge, or glittering spear
'Tis not, Death! thy bitter chalice
   Makes the sleeping infant fear.
'Tis the ingratitude of mortals,
   Darker far than tyrant's art,
Reaches with its pointed arrow
   Even the Messiah's heart.

HYMN TO MARY.

CHORUS.

STAR of the ocean!
Mid life's commotion,
We, with devotion,
   Follow thy light.
Keep us still wary,
Lest we may vary;
Mary! Sweet Mary!
Guide us aright.

O spotless Queen of Virgins!
  With shining lilies crowned,
Grant, we, thy youthful daughters,
  May pure, like thee, be found.
          Star of the ocean, &c.

Thou art the Queen of Martyrs,
  Crowned when thy Jesus died;
May I, thy sorrows sharing,
  Weep with thee side by side.
          Star of the ocean, &c.

To wretched mortals ever,
  Thou gentle art and kind,
In thee support and refuge,
  Repentant sinners find.
          Star of the ocean, &c.

3*

I know that all thy glories
  No human tongue can tell;
And still, my own sweet mother!
  ·I know I love thee well.
           Star of the ocean, &c.

Oh, save my soul, Blest Lady!
  In Heaven with God and thee,
That I may love and praise thee
  For all eternity.
           Star of the ocean, &c.

A CHILD'S MAY SONG.

FROM thy bright throne above the sky,
  Look down on us, O Mother sweet,
And smile upon the gift which I
  Here offer kneeling at thy feet.

Mother of my God and mine,
  I've brought some simple flowers to-day,
That they may bloom upon thy shrine
  The long, long hours that I'm away.

So their sweet breath shall rise like prayer,
  When I am far from this dear spot;
Thou'lt think of me while they are here,
  And absent, I'll forget thee not.

If I were rich in gems and gold,
  All, all to thee I'd freely give;
How could I any thing withhold
  That it might please thee to receive?

But if I had a golden mine,
  And were to lay it at thy feet;
My heart not being truly thine,
  Say, would it please thee, Mother sweet?

I know it would not, and I know
  That I can only be thine own,
By loving Him who loved thee so
  That He became thine own dear son.

My heart henceforth shall be all thine,
  And I will watch, and I will pray,
That never thought or word of mine,
  May take my heart from thee away.

Oh! give a blessing now to me,
  I'll try to be so good all day,
That I may bring fresh flowers to thee,
  To make thy sweet white altar gay.

THE TEAR OF INNOCENCE.

THE tear of innocence—how bright
   It gushes from the eye,
It wins the sympathy of men,
   The blessings of the sky.
Before the tender infant's tongue
   Has learned to shape a sound,
It tells with simple eloquence
   His little wants around.

It droppeth from a daughter's eye
   Upon a mother's bier,
And with the spirit-world it links
   The gentle mourner here.
At Misery's piercing voice it wells
   Up from the feeling heart,
And gives the homeless wanderer,
   What gold could ne'er impart.

When Saints, remote from mortal gaze,
   Bend low in fervent prayer;
The language of the soul to God
   Is still the unbidden tear.
It fell in Bethlehem's grot—and, borne
   By Mercy up to Heaven,
Of Justice on his throne obtained,
   That man should be forgiven.

PURGATORY.

SPIRITS that languish,
  In cleansing fire,
Great is your anguish,
  As your desire!
We who could lend you
  Aid and relief,
Fail to befriend you,
  Leave you to grief.

When gentle showers
  Cool the parched beds,
Languishing flowers
  Lift up their heads.
Christ's precious merits,
  Like gentle rain,
Soothe the good spirits,
  In their great pain.

To the dim region,
  Where dear ones mourn,
Love and religion
  Bid us oft turn.
Prayer hath the power
  To give them peace,
Speeding the hour
  Of their release.

A NIGHT PRAYER.

GREAT GOD, I call upon thy name,
   And bow before thy throne,
Amid the silent shades of night,
   Unwatched, unseen, alone.
How oft amidst the glare of day,
   When pleasure's throng was nigh,
I have forgotten that I moved
   Beneath thy watchful eye!

Mine eyes have dwelt on vanities,
   Thy children should not see;
My feet forsook the pleasant paths,
   That lead to Heaven, to Thee.
I kneel and humbly own my sin,
   With many a tear and prayer;
My soul hath dwelt 'mid earthly joys,
   And found no pleasure there.

I know, I feel, my own dear Lord!
   I ne'er can happy be,
Unless my soul shall centre all
   Its hopes, its love in thee.
Be faithful, then, my wayward heart!
   Let worldly joys grow dim;
Thou'rt made for God, and never wilt,
   Find rest unless in Him.

SONG OF THE UNION.

ERE Peace and Freedom, hand in hand,
Went forth to bless this happy land,
  And make it their abode,
It was the footstool of a throne;
But now no master here is known,
  No King is feared but God.

Americans uprose in might,
And triumphed in th' unequal fight,
  For Union made them strong:—
Union! the magic battle-cry
That hurled the tyrant from on high,
  And crushed his hireling throng!

That word since then hath shone on high
In starry letters to the sky—
  It is our country's name!
What impious hand shall rashly dare
Down from its lofty peak to tear
  The banner of her fame?

The spirits of th' heroic dead,
Who for Columbia fought and bled,
  Would curse the dastard son,
Who should betray their noble trust,
And madly trample in the dust,
  The charter which they won.

From vast Niagara's gurgling roar
To Sacramento's golden shore,
   From east to western wave,
The blended vows of millions rise,
Their voice re-echoes to the skies—
   "The Union we must save!"

The God of nations, in whose name
The sacred laws obedience claim,
   Will bless our fond endeavor
To dwell as brethren here below—
The Union then, come weal, come woe,
   We will preserve forever!

THE BLESSED EUCHARIST.

THY power, O Lord, is boundless power,
   Thy love is boundless love;
And for that love and by that power
   Thou comest from above.
        Son of God! we bow before thee
        Blessed Saviour! we adore thee.

Beneath the outward forms of bread,
   That seems but is not here,
The living manna lies concealed,
   The Lamb of God is near.
        Son of God! we bow before thee,
        Blessed Saviour! we adore thee.

We cannot see thee, yet we know
  Thou'rt present, dearest Lord;
'Tis not the sight that guides our mind—
  'Tis faith in thy true word.
      Son of God! we bow before thee,
      Blessed Saviour! we adore thee.

Were all the beauty of thy face
  Unveiled to mortal sight,
We'd fall to earth; we could not bear
  The blaze of heaven's full light.
      Son of God! we bow before thee,
      Blessed Saviour! we adore thee.

Come, Lord, to me, and all my heart
  Shall be fore'er thine own,
And I shall care and I shall sigh
  For thee—for thee alone.
      Son of God! we bow before thee,
      Blessed Saviour! we adore thee.

Thy love for me, and mine for thee,
  In one bright flame now burns,
And thus thy love for my poor soul
  To thee, sweet Lord, returns.
      Son of God! we bow before thee,
      Blessed Saviour! we adore thee.

O bread of angels, food of life,
   Be thou my life, my love,
My strength and comfort here below,
   My joy in heaven above.
      Son of God! we bow before thee,
      Blessed Saviour! we adore thee.

CHILD'S HYMN TO THE GUARDIAN ANGEL.

How kind it is of you to come,
Bright angel, from your starry home,
And watch by night and watch by day,
Beside a sinful child of clay!
How good and pure I ought to be,
Who always live so near to thee,
Beneath thine eyes the whole day round,
Where'er I tread is holy ground.

And if I had my wish I would,
Dear angel mine! be always good,
This minute I would rather die,
Than say bad words or tell a lie.
I always feel disposed this way,
Whene'er I kneel me down to pray,
But I forget when church is o'er,
And am as naughty as before.

Oh blessed guardian, kind and mild,
Have pity on a poor weak child,
And pray that God will make me strong,
To do the right and shun the wrong.
Whenever I commit a sin,
I feel my very heart within
Grow chill and heavy like a clod,
Because I have offended God.

But I would love to fear the Lord,
And shun each sinful deed and word,
Not do the sin, then feel the force
Of bitter shame and keen remorse.
I wish to think of God and thee
Whenever pretty things I see,
Till every flower that gems the sod
Shall make me think of thee and God.

Inspired by faith, I wish to hear,
Thy gentle footfall strike my ear;
Before thy radiant face to bow,
And feel thy kiss upon my brow.
Thy broad white wings shall be my shield,
While battling on life's dusty field;
Thine arms enfold me when I die,
And waft me homeward to the sky.

HYMN OF THE CRUSADERS.

FROM "I LOMBARDI," BY VERDI.

O Signore dal tetto natio.

LORD OF HOSTS! from the home of our childhood
  Thou hast called us with promises holy,
We marched boldly through waste and through
    wildwood,
    Sure to conquer, yet ready to die.
  But our looks are dejected and lowly,
And thy servants are bowed down with sorrow.
Shall the cross and its warriors to-morrow
    Prove a scoff when the Paynim draw nigh?
We remember dear Lombardy's mountains,
  Her vineyards, her fields rich in glory,
Her fresh breezes, her murmuring fountains,
    The green bowers that wave in her land.
Ah! fond mem'ry, thou'rt scarcely a blessing,
  Thou recallest our childhood's sweet story,
But we're roused from thy dreamy caressing,
    By the glow of the hot desert sand.

HYMN OF THE HEBREWS.

FROM "NABUCO," BY VERDI.

Va pensiero sull' all dorate

Haste, fond mem'ry, thy vigor recalling,
Haste away to the valleys and mountains,
Where the breeze o'er Judea's bright fountains
Cools the air of our dear native land.

Hover fondly o'er Jordan's clear waters,
Mark the turrets of Sion now falling;
Oh! Judea, thy sons and thy daughters
Weep for thee on this barbarous strand.

Harp of gold! hast thou parted with glory,
That thou hangest unstrung on the willow?
Oh! as billow rolls on after billow,
Let the music rush o'er thy bright chords.

Dark and sad, like poor Solyma's story,
Breathe a dirge mixed with deep sighs of sor-
    row,
Or from mem'ry some bright ditty borrow,
Bearing courage and strength in its words.

4*

RECOLLECTION.

AIR—*O Signore dal tetto natio.*

FAR from Eden in exile we wander,
    'Mid the deep gloom of night and of error;
And of dreams we grow fonder and fonder,
    If we call not, O Lord, on thy power.
While we pray, every vision of terror
    Melts away like the dew-drops at morning,
And the wiles of the proud tempter scorning,
    We are free as in Eden's lost bower.

Oh this world when it scatters its flowers,
    When it gathers its trophies around me,
May beguile for a few fleeting hours,
    But the heart, Lord, is wretched, or thine.
Then before death has spread his dark pinion,
    And the spell of its shadow has bound me,
Let me bow to my Saviour's dominion,
    Let his glory or cross still be mine!

ENCOURAGEMENT.

AIR— *Va pensiero sull'ali dorate.*

SOUL, awaken, in sadness why languish?
    Break away from thy fears and thy fetters,
Feel the courage that rouses and betters,
    Leave the desert its silence and gloom.

Look abroad, honest work has its beauty,
  Earnest hearts can forget their own anguish,
And can toil in the vineyard of duty,
  While the sluggard sits wailing his doom.

Saddest hearts 'neath their ashes have embers,
  That will glow if we do good to others;
For the prayers of our needier brothers,
  Turn to blessings and follow us home.

We are all of one body the members,
  Here to-day be we sharers in sorrow;
For we hope to be sharers to-morrow,
  In the light of the glory to come.

TO THE EVER BLESSED TRINITY.

ALMIGHTY Sire! I am dust,
Unbounded power is thine;
Weakness and want are mine,
In thee my love, my trust.

CHORUS.

Sanctus Deus,
Sanctus fortis,
Sanctus immortalis,
Miserere nobis!

Eternal Son! I am blind,
The light of light is thine;
Error and doubt are mine,
Guide thou my trembling mind.
    CHORUS—Sanctus Deus, etc.

Oh Holy Ghost! Give heart,
All life, all love are thine,
Frailty and grief are mine,
To me thy warmth impart.
    CHORUS—Sanctus Deus, etc.

HYMN TO THE HOLY GHOST.

GOD the Holy Ghost! Lifegiver!
    Of the Three Blest Persons Third,
Humbly kneeling we adore thee,
    With the Father and the Word.
Thou art of the selfsame nature,
    As the Father and the Son,
Equally from both proceeding,
    Thou dost bind them both in One.

They distinct in person only,
    Into thee breathe life divine;
And the essence of the Godhead,
    Flows into their life from thine.

In the far eternal ages,
  With the Father and the Word,
Thou didst reign in might and glory,
  Equal God and equal Lord.

Life and love have their beginning,
  And they have their end in thee;
Life cannot endure without thee,
  Love without thee cannot be.
Thou hast spoken by the Prophets
  In Judea's favored land,
While they wrote the sacred pages,
  Thou hast guided mind and hand.

Thou didst clothe the Word Eternal
  With our flesh in Mary's womb,
When he came from heaven to save us
  From our sinful parents' doom.
Like a dove near Jordan's waters,
  Hov'ring o'er the promised one,
Madest known to Jew and Gentile,
  God's beloved only Son.

When the chosen Twelve lay hidden,
  From Judea's watchful ire,
They beheld and felt thee coming,
  In the form of tongues of fire.

Boldly from the upper chamber,
  By thee led they sallied forth,
Preaching Christ and working wonders,
  In all regions of the earth.

Holy Spirit, in thy beauty
  Ever ancient, ever new,
Guard the Church which thou hast founded,
  Keep her children firm and true.
Never let us sin against thee,
  Paraclete! we trust in thee!
With thy fruits and gifts surround us,
  'Till thy face in heaven we see.

HYMN OF PRAISE.

LORD! when a silvery star
Gleams in the blue depths afar,
Thoughts come to me of thine eye
Looking on us from the sky.
Lord! when a tremulous beam
Sleeps on the shadowy stream,
Thoughts come to me of thy love,
Brightening our hearts from above.

Chorus.

All that is winning and fair,
Speaks of thy love and thy care;
All that is noble and grand,
Speaks of the power of thy hand.
All things are made by thy word,
All thy works praise thee, O Lord;
Gladly our voices we raise,
Joining the hymn of thy praise.

If to the hills I retreat,
There I find prints of thy feet;
Down in the caves of the sea,
Coral and gems tell of thee.
Deep in the shadowy wood,
Deer for their young ones get food;
Wolves even find in their lair,
Proofs of thy pitying care.

Chorus—All that is winning, etc.

Cheered by thy dew and thy rain,
Orchard and field bloom again;
All the bright flowers are by thee,
Scattered o'er hillock and lea.
There's not a fish in the seas,
There's not a bird in the trees,

Thou dost not reach with thine eyes,
From thy bright throne in the skies.

CHORUS—All that is winning, etc,

Children of God, all your days,
Joyfully sing in his praise;
Saints and bright spirits above,
Tell of his goodness and love.
All that is noble and fair,
Tells of his power and his care;
Joyfully sing in his praise,
Children of God, all your days.

CHORUS—All that is winning, etc.

HYMN OF TRUST.

O BRIGHTNESS of eternal light,
  I worship at thy feet;
Though all unworthy in thy sight,
  Thy mercies I repeat.
To save our souls from sin and strife,
  Is still thy work divine;
The gates of everlasting life,
  Are thine, O Lord, are thine.

I love to praise thee when the sun
   Pours forth his early light,
And when the bright stars one by one
   Come twinkling out at night.
If I am free from care and loss,
   I love to praise thy name;
If I am called to bear thy cross,
   I bless thee all the same.

If roses on my path I meet,
   I feel the gift is thine;
If briers spring to pierce my feet,
   I strive to ne'er repine.
The blessings sent to win my love,
   O Lord, I freely take;
The trials sent my faith to prove,
   I bear for thy dear sake.

Let favoring winds and friendly waves,
   Speed on my little bark;
Or let me sail where ocean raves,
   And skies are chill and dark:
Let fortune smile, or let her frown,
   Let good or ill betide,
I know and feel I'm not alone,
   For thou art by my side.

5

Then I shall on my journey go,
　And fear not for the end;
It matters not who is my foe,
　If Jesus is my friend.
In thee, sweet Lord, I put my trust,
　O guard me while I live;
And when this dust returns to dust,
　My soul in heaven receive.

THANKSGIVING.

A HYMN of thanksgiving
　Lift up to the Lord;
Whatever is living,
　Hath life by his word.
Though made without merit,
　By mercy alone,
Our soul is a spirit,
　Resembling his own.

CHORUS.

With souls true and tender,
　With hearts glad and free,
Great Father! we render,
　Devout thanks to thee.

We bow down before thee,
    And fervently pray,
To love and adore thee,
    Forever and aye.

The life which he gave us,
    He guards for us still;
He watches to save us,
    From error and ill.
The dew falls from heaven,
    The grain and the fruit
In season are given,
    Our strength to recruit.

CHORUS—With souls true, etc.

When dangers alarm us,
    He comforts our hearts;
When demons would harm us,
    He baffles their arts.
When Doubt seeks to madden
    With thoughts of despair,
His Grace shines to gladden,
    With hopes bright and fair.

CHORUS—With souls true, etc.

Each bright smile that dwelleth,
  With us in our homes,
Of God's mercy telleth,
  Since from him it comes.
Our father and mother
  He gave, and our friends ;
His love, and none other,
  All good to us sends.

CHORUS—With souls true, etc.

His are the green bowers,
  Where summer birds sing,
The beautiful flowers,
  That gladden the spring ;
The murmuring fountain,
  The cool breeze of morn,
The forest-clad mountain,
  The bright field of corn.

CHORUS—With souls true, etc.

He sends Faith that traces,
  The only true way,
And thousands of graces,
  That crown us each day.

Thus God here caresses,
  His servants and friends;
And evermore blesses
  Their souls when life ends.

CHORUS—With souls true, etc.

HOPE.

WHEN the air is
  Warm and bright,
Think of God who
  Made the light.
If the tempest
  Should draw nigh,
Children, fear not,
  'Twill go by.
Children, fear not,
  'Twill go by.

When your heart is
  Full of glee,
Think of God who
  Makes you free.

5*

If some grief is
   O'er you cast,
Children, fear not,
   'Twill not last.
Children, fear not,
   'Twill not last.

If your friends are
   Firm and true,
Think of God, who
   Gave them you.
If you're helpless
   In your home,
Children, doubt not,
   Friends will come.
Children, doubt not,
   Friends will come.

If you're blest with
   Blooming health,
Think of God, who
   Gave such wealth.
If some ailment
   Try your heart,
Children, grieve not,
   'Twill depart.
Children, grieve not,
   'Twill depart.

While your life is
To you spared,
Think of God, who
For you cared.
If pale Death is
At your doors,
Children, weep not,
Heaven is yours.
Children, weep not,
Heaven is yours.

———

COMMUNION OF CHILDREN.

WHAT light is streaming from the skies,
Revealing heaven to mortal eyes,
What voice is singing from the spheres,
Angelic hymns to mortal ears?
O holiest mystery of love!
From his resplendent throne above,
The Saviour comes unseen to dwell,
Among the souls he loveth well.

He cometh not in fiery cloud,
He speaketh not in thunder loud;
He looseth not the storm-wind's breath,
To frighten men with fear of death.

But as he is in heaven above,
He comes in beauty and in love,
To fill with sweetest peace, and cheer
The hearts his own heart holds so dear.

Your soul must be as white as snow,
When to the mystic feast you go,
There to receive—O heavenly bliss!
Upon your lips the Saviour's kiss.
You will become his happy guest,
A flood of joy shall fill your breast;
All earthly cares shall fade away,
As night before the approach of day.

The bread of angels will impart
New vigor to your mind and heart;
You will become a child of truth,
Endowed with everlasting youth.
New virtues in you shall abound,
Like flowers of spring in goodly ground;
The Lord is with you! his right arm
Shall guard your future life from harm.

O happy soul, O happy soul,
Thy race is sure and heaven the goal;
Thy Saviour loveth thee so well,
That he is come with thee to dwell.

O thou art like an Angel now,
Cloud not with sin thy radiant brow;
Live on in hope and purity,
And God will give his heaven to thee.

ST. JOSEPH.

HIS SORROWS AND JOYS.

I.

JOSEPH thinks to part with Mary,
Doubt perplexes him and grieves him,
But an Angel's voice relieves him,
   And explains the mystery.

   Dear St. Joseph, I implore thee,
   By the sorrows that oppressed thee,
   By the many joys that blessed thee,
     Dear, St. Joseph, pray for me.

II.

Seeing Christ in Bethelem's manger,
Sorrow fills his heart so tender ;
He's consoled by sudden splendor,
   And celestial melody.

   Dear St. Joseph, etc.

III.

Joseph weeps, he has to witness
Jesus in the temple bleeding;
But is cheered the future reading
 In Old Simeon's prophecy.
  Dear St. Joseph, etc.

IV.

Now they fly from ruthless Herod,
And our Saint is filled with sadness;
Angels soon bring light and gladness,
 To the Holy Family.
  Dear St. Joseph, etc.

V.

Jesus lost! and vainly seeking,
His fond parents droop and languish;
But they soon forget their anguish,
 In their Saviour's company.
  Dear St. Joseph, etc.

VI.

Joseph mourns o'er man forgetful,
Of his Saviour near and present;
Yet his home is sweet and pleasant,
 Jesus shares his poverty.
  Dear St. Joseph, etc.

VII.

Now the Patriarch is dying,
'Tis the hour for sad leave-taking;
Jesus comforts him, awaking
  Thoughts of blest Eternity.
    Dear St. Joseph, etc.

ST. FRANCIS DE SALES.

OFTENTIMES when angry billows
  Surge and toss upon the main,
They are beaten down and vanquished,
  By a soft and steady rain.
So the gentle words of Francis
  Fell upon a warlike age;
So his virtues sweet and patient,
  Tempered Passion's gloomy rage.

Meekness made his soul her dwelling,
  From the days of early youth;
Yet as stands a rock-built tower,
  Firm he stood for right and truth.
For the alternate joys and sorrows
  Of the Priesthood set apart,
He combined a Martyr's courage,
  With a gentle Virgin's heart.

Why did countless unbelievers
  Round the holy Prelate crowd?
Why did sinners at his preaching
  Raise their voice and weep aloud?
'Twas the loving soul within him,
  Shining through his form and face,
Drew his yielding willing hearers
  To his fatherly embrace.

Pure in all things as an Angel,
  Fond and simple as a child,
With himself severe and watchful,
  With the poor and fallen mild;
He proclaimed that passion leads us
  O'er a dark and thorny road,
And that men are happy only
  When they love and serve their God.

Holy Francis, now in heaven,
  Sweetly guide thy children still,
To a life of true devotion,
  Free from doubt and free from ill.
Let the love of God inspire us,
  Let all earthly joys grow dim,
So that we may learn to suffer,
  Learn to live and die for him.

ST. JANE FRANCES DE CHANTAL.

JANE DE CHANTAL, worthy pupil
  Of the great and good De Sales,
Thee our song with pious homage,
  On this festal morning hails.
Nurtured in thy father's castle,
  When a sweet and gentle girl;
Thou wert never spoiled by grandeur,
  Nor by fashion's giddy whirl.

On the shining star of duty
  Ever dwelt thy watchful eye,
For thy hope and love were centred
  In thy home beyond the sky.
Happy was the gallant baron,
  He who claimed thee for his bride;
Thou wert of his home the treasure,
  Of his race the flower and pride.

And yet thou, O sainted Lady,
  Peace and pardon didst award,
To the friend whose careless weapon
  Put to death thy noble Lord.
Ah, the Saints of God were ever
  Truly humble, truly meek;
Let us learn from their example,
  Never for revenge to seek.

6

In a bright and happy household,
    Passed thy useful widowhood;
There thy children grew up round thee,
    Like their mother, pure and good.
Yet from ties so dear and tender,
    From the friends that loved thee well,
Jesus drew thee gently onward,
    To the cloister and the cell.

Called by heaven, many daughters
    Soon were gathered in thy school;
Many still, from every nation,
    Bless thy wise and loving rule.
Holy Foundress, let thy spirit
    Guide us on the upward road;
Let us, walking in thy footsteps,
    " Die to self and live to God."

ST. VINCENT DE PAUL.

A HYMN to St. Vincent de Paul,
    The Apostle of brotherly love!
He cared for the great and the small,
    As sons of one Father above.
He taught men in Luxury's dome,
    The wisdom that feareth the Lord;
He taught men in Poverty's home,
    The patience that trusts in His word.

From parents by want driven wild,
   From bye-ways for crime set apart,
He gathered the shivering child,
   And cradled it next his warm heart.
From snares but too artfully laid,
   By bold men and bad men of earth,
He rescued the innocent maid,
   And led her to honor and worth.

The floor of the dungeon he trod,
   Mid outcries of anguish and spite;
The smile of the servant of God,
   O'er hearts that were hopeless shed light.
He from the dark river hard by,
   Drew back the poor victim of shame;
He bade her look up to the sky,
   And hope in the all-saving Name.

The Daughters of Vincent de Paul
   Went forth on their mission of love,
They are sisters to each one and all
   Who are dear to Our Father above.
Whenever a crime or an ill
   Dims the image and likeness divine,
They are guided by Charity still,
   To watch where the wretched recline.

What suffering of fallen mankind
  Has Vincent passed by or forgot?
Where failed he with heart and with mind
  To better Humanity's lot?
Then love him, and pray God to send,
  Your life may resemble his own;
See in each man a brother, a friend,
  Love sinners, and hate sin alone.

ST. MARY MAGDALEN.

O MAGDALEN! O Magdalen,
  I see thee in the Supper Hall,
I hear the sob thou gavest then,
  I see the tear-drop gush and fall.
A sorrow something like thy own,
  Is busy in my sinful heart;
But while I sigh and while I moan,
  I feel I am not what thou art.

O Magdalen, O Magdalen,
  I see thee Penitent and Blest,
And ask my guilty conscience when
  It will consent to give me rest!
I ceased to fight 'gainst Sin and Hell,
  I drank the World's empoisoned cup,
And found he must in misery dwell,
  Who meanly gives the battle up.

O Magdalen, O Magdalen,
  Thy Saviour saw thy grief, thy love;
He blessed thee and forgave thee then,
  He sees me now from heaven above.
Thou standest near his throne—oh pray,
  Dear Saint! and let thy prayer be such,
That I, unworthy sinner, may,
  Be pardoned too by loving much.

ST. TERESA.

VIRGIN daughter of Castile,
  All thy country's olden worth,
All her knightly fire and zeal,
  Burned within thee from thy birth.
Ah, the world with cunning art,
  Strove its idols to enthrone,
In the warm and noble heart,
  God had formed to be his own.

Thou wert led from love so vain,
  Thou wert scourged with sorrow's rod,
And thy body drooped with pain,
  But thy soul rose nearer God.
He consoles thy spirit now,
  With a sense of joyful rest;
Heavenly wisdom bathes thy brow,
  Heavenly rapture fills thy breast.
6*

Now a dryness and a gloom
  O'er thee pass and try thy love,
Soon they vanish—light hath come,
  Dew hath fallen from above.
Let the world annoy thee sore,
  And with thorns thy pathway sow,
Jesus braved its scorn before,
  Wore its thorns upon his brow.

Far away from worldly strife,
  And forgetting human care,
Thou didst live a higher life,
  Nourished by the food of prayer.
See! the Angel hovers near,
  With his mystic fiery dart,
Heavenly music fills thine ear,
  Heavenly love has pierced thy heart.

Neither earth nor heaven to thee
  Could a dearer joy afford,
Than in mind and heart to be
  Still united with thy Lord.
Teach thy children how we may
  Know him, love him, serve him here,
And behold his face one day,
  In a better, higher sphere.

MARY, HELP OF CHRISTIANS.

HELP of Christians, while the combat
Deepens round us, we beseech thee,
Let our prayerful voices reach thee,
　　Grant us succor lest we fall.
Life on earth is ceaseless warfare,
Many fears and cares oppress us,
Many bitter foes distress us,
　　Thou wilt save us from them all.

First the artful world allures us,
All its wealth before us flaunting,
Of its ease and freedom vaunting,
　　Of its pomps and vanity.
Woe to us if we are dazzled,
By its boldness and profusion,
Time dispels the world's illusion,
　　Death unveils its treachery.

Next the Devil would ensnare us,
Of a godlike wisdom telling,
Man might conquer by rebelling,
　　'Gainst the laws of Truth and Right.
Woe if Doubt and Pride should lead us,
Into Satan's fatal error,
Life would be a day of terror,
　　Death a mute and starless night.

Last the Flesh gives baneful counsel,
Whispering of a life of pleasure,
Without end and without measure,
   Where its languid votaries dwell.
Woe if we by sense are blinded,
Life in idle pastime spending
We should barter bliss unending,
   For vain joys that lead to hell.

Help of Christians, while the combat
Deepens round us, we beseech thee
Let our prayerful voices reach thee,
   Grant us succor lest we fall.
Life on earth is ceaseless warfare,
Many fears and cares oppress us,
Many bitter foes distress us,
   Thou wilt save us from them all.

THE MONTH OF MARY.

Snow and rain have vanished,
   Winds have ceased to wail,
Gloomy winter's banished
From the hill and dale.

CHORUS.

Gentle Mother hear us,
At thy altar pray,
Queen of Saints, be near us
On this sweet May-day.

Spring hath come with flowers,
  Spring hath come with light,
Soft and rosy hours
  Fill the day and night.

CHORUS—Gentle Mother, etc.

Stars above us gleaming,
  Tell of Mary's worth,
Blossoms 'round us teeming,
  Speak her praise to earth.

CHORUS—Gentle Mother, etc.

Here below deserving
  She was found alone,
God from sin preserving,
  Chose her for his own.

CHORUS—Gentle Mother, etc.

Grace as to none other,
  Grace to her was given,
She became the mother,
  Of the King of heaven.

> CHORUS—Gentle Mother, etc.

God bestowed upon her
  Glories all her own,
Earth's sublimest honor,
  Heaven's queenly throne.

> CHORUS—Gentle Mother, etc.

Taught by Him we love her,
  In our simple way,
Placing none above her,
  On this sweet May-day.

> CHORUS—Gentle Mother, etc.

THE LORD'S DAY.

CHORUS.

THIS is the day our Lord
  Hath chosen for his own;
Come, mortals, from your toil,
  And worship at his throne.

Lift up your hearts in prayer,
   And let your wants be known;
This is the day our Lord,
   Hath chosen for his own.

The Lord made heaven and earth,
   The stars, the moon, the sun,
And on the seventh day,
   His wondrous work was done.
In six days all were made,
   The seventh day he blessed,
Because his work was o'er,
   And this the day of rest,

   CHORUS—This is the day, etc.

From Sinai's burning mount
   The Lord's commands were given,
And Israel shook with fear,
   To hear the voice of heaven.
" The Sabbath-day is mine,"
   That voice was heard to say,
" Let all the people know,
   And keep the Sabbath-day."

   CHORUS—This is the day, etc.

When Jesus came himself
   Our erring souls to seek,
He made the Sabbath-day
   The first day of the week;
That day the Saviour blessed,
   His glorious work was done,
And heaven's eternal rest,
   That day became our own.

      CHORUS—This is the day, etc.

THE CHILD JESUS.

AT night the wealthy citizen
   Had turned him from the door,
The only friends around him were
   The lowly and the poor.
Yet to his Father's will resigned,
   The new-born infant smiled:
This came to pass in Bethlehem,
   When Jesus was a child.

He came to do his Father's work,
   His Father's law to teach;
The Jewish doctors wondered at
   The wisdom of his speech.

In giving reasons for his faith,
　The hours away he whiled :
This came to pass in Solyma,
　When Jesus was a child.

Beneath Saint Joseph's humble roof,
　He with his mother dwelt ;
His gentle words revealed to them,
　The love his bosom felt.
In every action he was kind,
　In manner always mild :
This came to pass in Nazareth,
　When Jesus was a child.

Have I been patient, wise, and good,
　When home and when abroad?
Ah no! too often I behaved
　Unlike a child of God.
In future, with my Father's will,
　I shall be reconciled,
And try to do as Jesus did,
　When Jesus was a child.

7

THE SEVEN ARCHANGELS.

THERE are seven bright spirits that stand
  Near the throne of Jehovah in heaven,
And to these seven spirits, command,
  Over all the good angels, is given.
They keep watch 'neath a banner of light,
  Upon God's holy mountain unrolled;
They are clad in full armor, so bright
  That it flashes like jewels and gold.

And their faces are gentle and fair,
  But their look and their bearing sublime,
As when Lucifer fled through the air,
  From their swords, in the far-away time.
During battle they pour on the field,
  The red vials of long-treasured wrath,
And the sword of bright flame which they wield,
  Smiteth conquering Pride on his path.

But these beautiful spirits draw near
  When the clouds of adversity frown;
And the soul of the martyr they cheer,
  For they bring him the palm and the crown.
And the traveler on life's weary way,
  Finds a shield in their heavenly might,
'Gainst the arrow that flieth by day,
  And the fiend that goes prowling by night.

As the sweet-smelling vapor ascends,
　From their censers before the Most High,
With the prayer of the just man it blends,
　And the sinful one's penitent sigh.
At our altars they worship unseen,
　Giving praise to their Lord through the night;
And the soul of the Christian they screen,
　When he fights at his death the last fight.

Great Saint Michael is chief in command
　O'er the hosts of the children of light,
Blessed Gabriel and Raphael stand
　Next in dignity, honor, and might.
All ye blessed Archangels, give ear
　To my earnest and suppliant prayer,
Let me live in the Lord's holy fear,
　And for judgment in season prepare.

MASS HYMN.

PART I.

Worship.

Most Holy Trinity, One God
　Supreme in majesty,
All power in heaven and earth is thine,
　All things belong to thee.

I offer up the Holy Mass,
  This morning, with the aim
Of blessing thy Almighty power,
  And worshipping thy name.

CHORUS.

By thy own Incarnate Word,
We adore thee, Blessed Lord.

PART II.

Thanksgiving.

Almighty and Eternal God,
  Thou art the good supreme;
Thou dost create us and preserve,
  Thou dost our souls redeem.
For these and all thy benefits,
  Thy mercy we adore,
And offer up the Holy Mass,
  To thank thee more and more.

CHORUS.

By thy own Incarnate Word,
We give thanks to thee, O. Lord.

PART III.

Atonement.

The merits of the Lamb of God,
    Can grace for all obtain;
His precious blood from every soul,
    Can wash out every stain.
I offer up his precious blood,
    To thee, my God, this day;
Oh! pardon us, and give us grace,
    No more to go astray.

CHORUS.

    Through thy own Incarnate Word,
    Grant us mercy, Blessed Lord.

PART IV.

Petition.

All men have need of thee, my God,
    The just that love thy name,
The souls that sleep in sin, and those
    That feel the cleansing flame.
O grant thy blessing and thy grace,
    To all for whom we pray;
For this, O Lord, we offer up,
    The Holy Mass to-day.

CHORUS.

    Through thy own Incarnate Word,
    Hear our prayer, O Blessed Lord.

7*

GOD SAVE THE COMMONWEALTH.

GOD of mercy, hear thy people,
  While they humbly pray before thee,
  By thy goodness, we implore thee,
Save, O Lord, the Commonwealth.

Bless the land with peace and plenty,
  Keep in brotherly communion
  All the States of all the Union,
Save, O Lord, the Commonwealth.

Teach us how to love our Country,
  All her righteous laws revering,
  Hating no one, no one fearing,
Save, O Lord, the Commonwealth.

Grant America thy blessing,
  Let her children in each region
  Cherish truth and love religion;
Save, O Lord, the Commonwealth.

On the land and on the ocean,
  Bless and guard our country's banner,
  Let it ever float with honor,
Save, O Lord, the Commonwealth.

Bless the Army and the Navy,
  Guard our commerce from disaster,
  Be our Father and our Master,
Save, O Lord, the Commonwealth.

THE HOLY INNOCENTS.

I HEAR a voice from Bethlehem,
  The moan of winds resembling,
It swelleth upward fitfully,
  Then falleth weakly trembling.·
'Tis Rachel mourning bitterly,
  Her young in cold death sleeping,
O'er Rama spreadeth drearily,
  The chorus of her weeping.

At eve the happy shepherdess
  Home from the pasture wended,
Upon the green slept peacefully,
  The little flock she tended.
Her faithful spouse, at eventide,
  Came gladly forth to meet her,
And bright as Rose of Jericho,
  Their infant smiled to greet her.

The midnight tramp of soldiery
  Wakes Bethlem's peaceful daughters,
A cruel tyrant's jealousy
  Dyes red old Jordan's waters.
Beneath the starlight wandering,
  Meanwhile the world's Redeemer,
Avoids the prowling satellite,
  And foils the royal schemer.

Oh, mothers of fair Bethlehem,
  God wills ye weep no longer,
The new-born king of Nazareth,
  Than all your foes is stronger.
He will return to Solyma,
  And smite the tyrant gory;
He to each martyred Innocent
  Will give a crown of glory.

DEW-DROPS OF WISDOM.

HEAR the word
Of the Lord,
While in youth
Learn the truth.
Youth is bold,
Ere yet cold,
Let the earth
Know its worth.

Let its sighs
Heavenward rise,
Be its love
Fixed above.
Always fight
For the right,
And be strong
'Gainst the wrong.

Be a child
Kind and mild,
Never rude,
Ever good.
Be not bold
With the old,
Do what's fair,
Everywhere.

Never swerve
Time to serve;
Never lie,
Rather die.
Well begun
Means half done,
Do your best,
Then seek rest.

If you make
A mistake,
Do not grieve,
But retrieve.
Should you fail,
Do not wail ;
That were vain,
Try again.

Kneel and pray
Every day,
In God's sight,
Morn and night.
Bravely own
To wrong done ;
Then you'll do
Good anew.

Try God's will
To fulfill,
By it stand
Heart and hand.
If you err,
Don't despair,
But correct
Your defect.

Help the poor,
And be sure
Of reward,
From the Lord.
Do not shirk
Honest work;
Earning food
Makes it good.

Never walk,
Pray, or talk,
With a lad
Who is bad.
Fear the Lord,
Love his word,
Keep his ways
All your days.

Every hour
Hath the power,
To annoy,
Or give joy.
Every day
Hath its say;
Days to come
All are dumb.

Do not fret
For them yet,
.   Learn best how
To live now.
If in haste
Time you'll waste,
So proceed
Slow with speed.

THE LANGUAGE OF FEELING.

I LOVE to see a tear-drop
    Stand trembling in the eye,
Not when rude sorrow's question
    Hath wrung the heart's reply ;
But when some gentle pity
    Hath softly called it up,
It sparkles like a dew-drop
    Within a violet's cup.

I love to see the sunlight
    That gilds a mantling blush,
Not when detected baseness
    Hath caused the cheek to flush ;
But when true modest instincts
    Sweep heart-strings in their reach,
It shines with artless beauty,
    Like glow on downy peach.

I love to see the grandeur
    That gathers with a frown,
Not when low pride or envy,
    Hath drawn its terrors down;
But roused by generous feeling
    'Gainst cruel deeds, or mean,
It brightens wrath as lightning
    Illumes a stormy scene.

I love to hear the music
    That gushes with a sigh,
Not when grief drives the wretched
    To wish that they might die;
But when we turn from pleasures
    This lower world hath given,
'Tis like a pinion's flutter
    That wafts the soul to heaven.

THE VOYAGE OF LIFE.

Upon the sea at morning,
The breeze and billow scorning,
    Youth gayly speeds away;
The birds are sweetly singing,
The early flowers are springing,
    It is the dawn of day.

8

The storm is darkly brewing,
And man his course pursuing,
  Must struggle or must die.
He perishes who prays not,
But he in grief delays not,
  Who seeks for aid on high.

The bark has long been sailing,
The light of day is failing,
  And age is near its doom.
But in the child of duty,
A smile of hope and beauty
  Sheds sunlight o'er the tomb.

Our bark the port is nearing,
Dear Angel Guardian steering,
  Oh, guide it on its road.
We love thee and obey thee,
Lead on, lead on, we pray thee,
  To heaven and to God.

DEATH.

THE vision, the vision of Death and its terrors,
Has made me look over my life and its errors;
  I think and I tremble to think of my sins.
The battle of life is more fierce as it closes,
He loses for earth and for heaven who loses,
  And he wins forever and ever who wins.

O, Angels and Saints, ye have passed the dim
    portal,
That leads human spirits to mansions immortal,
  Be near when the last day of earth is at hand.
Remind us to turn from the world that would
    please us,
And hope in the name and the merits of Jesus,
  Your combat is over, and with Him ye stand.

Ah! He is my Father, and He is my Master;
My soul He will rescue from gloom and disaster.
  He told me to watch, and he taught me to
    pray;
He made me to live and to love him forever.
Shall I cease to hope in him? Never, oh,
    never!
  I'll trust in his goodness till life ebbs away.

THE ANGEL AND THE CHILD.*

An Angel bent over a cradle,
  And seemed to behold mirrored there
The light of his beautiful features,
  As though in a brook, still and fair.

* From the French of Reboul.

"Sweet Infant," thus gently he murmured,
   "Thou'rt like me—oh, come thou with me!
Away! we'll be happy together;
   This earth is not worthy of thee.

"The pleasures of earth are not lasting,
   They seek to enchant, but in vain,
For often bright smiles and gay laughter
   Are veils to hide passion and pain.
On days set apart for rejoicing,
   The soul may be weary and worn,
The sun, though it sets in its glory,
   Is shrouded with storm-clouds at morn.

"Shall traces of anguish and hatred
   Profane thy young brow still so clear?
Those blue eyes, so loving and tender—
   Are they to be dimmed by a tear?
Oh, no! let us fly hence together—
   Thy course shall be upward with mine;
For God, in his mercy, has spared thee
   The days that were yet to be thine.

"No mourners shall darken thy dwelling—
   No requiem lull thee to rest;
For those who are sinless as thou art,
   The last day of earth is the best."

The Angel thus ended his ditty ;
  But now his bright wings he has spread,
He soars ! he has gone back to heaven—
  Poor mother ! thy infant is dead !

———

THE VIRTUES AT BETHLEHEM.

WHEN the lowly grot of Bethlehem
  First received the holy child,
On the shepherds' humble offering
  The Redeemer kindly smiled ;
Faith, and Hope, and gentle Charity—
  Those three sisters pure and fair—
Were then led by light from heaven,
  To approach and worship there.

" Hail ! thou oracle of prophets,"
  Faith advancing, said, " All hail !"
From these eyes, once dim and blinded,
  Thou hast now removed the veil."
Hope then said, " At length I see thee
  Whom th' eternal hills desired,
And my sigh hast changed to gladness,
  Thou for whom my soul aspired."
8*

But when Charity there kneeling,
  With her downcast eyes and meek,
The devotion of her spirit
  In low tones essayed to speak,
Her sweet voice was lost in murmurs,
  And for words she vainly strove,
So she kissed the sacred forehead,
  Weeping tears of joy and love.

THE HOUR OF PRAYER.

PRELUDE.

(Some voices.)

It is the hour, it is the hour of Prayer,
Forget the earth, forget all earthly care;
Before the Lord of Heaven and Earth bow down
With simple hearts, and worship at his throne.

ADORATION.

(All—pianissimo.)

Father Almighty,
  We are but dust;
In thy great mercy
  We put our trust.

Thou art our Maker—
Thou art our Lord;
By men and angels
Thou art adored.

PRELUDE.

SUPPLICATION.

(*All—a little louder.*)

God of our fathers,
  Stretch forth thine arm;
Thou, who didst make us,
  Shield us from harm.
Teach us to name thee
  With sacred awe—
Teach us to love thee,
  And keep thy law.

PRELUDE.

PRAISE.

(*All—loud, and with joy.*)

Hear us, O Father,
  Father of all,
While with devotion
  On thee we call.

Look on thy children—
  Guard us always;
Render us worthy
  To sing thy praise.

———

QUEEN OF ANGELS.

CHILD'S HYMN.

Queen of Angels,
  Pray for me,
For my heart is
  Full of thee.
Thou art nearest
  God on high—
First and fairest
  In the sky.

Blessed Mary,
  Thy sweet name
Warms my bosom
  Like a flame.
Thy dear image
  When I kiss,
All my soul is
  Rapt in bliss.

Dost thou hear us
　When we pray—
When we bless thee
　Every day?
Yes! our Saviour
　Loves thee so,
He will surely
　Let thee know.

When we offer
　Flowers to thee,
He will surely
　Let thee see.
Thou his Mother,
　He thy Son,
What thou wishest
　Must be done.

Thou can'st never
　Try in vain
Grace or favor
　To obtain.
Thy dear Jesus
　Cannot choose
His sweet Mother
　To refuse.

Blessed Virgin,
　Pray for me,
Sailing on this
　Stormy sea;
Lead me onward
　Through the strife—
Guide me safe to
　Endless life.

SALUTATION TO MARY.

DAUGHTER of God the Father,
　O Virgin pure and mild,
I venerate and love thee—
　Accept me for thy child.
My soul, and all its powers,
　I consecrate to thee—
Be pleased, most holy Mother,
　From sin to keep me free.

CHORUS.

Be pleased, most holy Mother,
　To pray our Lord for me.

Mother of our Redeemer,
　O Virgin pure and mild,
I venerate and love thee—
　Accept me for thy child.

My body and its senses
　I consecrate to thee—
Be pleased, most holy Mother,
　From sin to keep me free.

CHORUS.

Be pleased, most holy Mother,
　To pray our Lord for me.

Spouse of the Holy Spirit,
　O Virgin, pure and mild,
I venerate and love thee—
　Accept me for thy child.
My heart and its affections
　I consecrate to thee—
Be pleased, most holy Mother,
　From sin to keep me free.

CHORUS.

Be pleased, most holy Mother,
　To pray our Lord for me.

HAPPY DEATH.

NEAR thy servant dying,
　Let thy Angel stand;
On thy grace relying,
　Let my heart expand.

When these eyes no longer
  See the light of earth,
Let my faith grow stronger—
  Shine with brighter worth.

Round thy servant dying,
  Let thy Saints draw near;
On thy grace relying,
  Let me cease to fear.
When all hope shall perish
  In the pow'r of men,
Firmer hope I'll cherish
  In thy power then.

On thy servant dying
  Let thy Mother smile;
On thy grace relying,
  I shall rest meanwhile.
When the light of Heaven
  Shineth from above,
All my sins forgiven,
  Let me die with love.

PRAYER OF DAVID.

Punish me not in the day of thy wrath—
Strike me not suddenly down in my path;

Let not the enemy laugh at my fall—
Pity me, Lord, who hast pity for all.
Judge of the fatherless, hope of the weak,
Refuge and help of the lowly and meek,
Look on my wretchedness, list to my grief,
Turn for thy mercy's sake, grant me relief.

Blessed the man who hath trust in the Lord,
He shall not fall by his enemy's sword;
He in his labors shall prosper and speed—
He shall prevail in the day of his need.
God giveth ear to the upright of heart—
God from his servants will never depart;
Hope from the morning watch even till night,
Hope in his mercy, and trust in his might.

Merciful Lord, thou hast heard me before—
Show forth thy goodness and glory once more;
Waters of sorrow have gathered 'round me—
Save me, O Father, my trust is in thee.
Thou wilt give ear to my suppliant prayer—
Thou wilt deliver my feet from the snare;
They that would wrong me shall hide in their
    shame,
While I give glory and praise to thy name.

9

THE VOICE OF CONSCIENCE.

YES! I have heard that whisper,
  That small still voice within;
It said: Take care, it said: Beware—
  Do not commit a sin.
I heeded not its warning,
  I wavered, and I fell,
And felt the force of stern Remorse
  That cowed me with its spell.
Thus fare I when I go to sin,
Nor heed the warning voice within.

Yes! I have heard that whisper,
  That small still voice within;
It said: Withdraw, break not the law—
  Thou art committing sin!
I heeded not its warning,
  But stubbornly kept on,
Till grace had fled, and faith was dead,
  And peace of mind was gone.
Thus fare I when I'm doing sin,
Nor heed the accusing voice within.

Yes! I have heard that whisper,
  That small still voice within;
It said: Thou'st warred against the Lord—
  Thou hast committed sin.

I heeded not its warning,
　　But walked my cheerless path,
In dread that God might seize the rod,
　　And smite me in his wrath.
Thus fare I when I've done a sin,
Nor heed the chiding voice within.

In future, when that whisper,
　　That small still voice within
Puts wrong and right before my sight,
　　And bids me not to sin,
I'll hearken to its warning
　　In every thought and deed,
Nor sin at all, or if I fall,
　　I will repent with speed.
Thus I shall keep me free from sin,
And heed the friendly voice within.

DEFINITIONS

AND

AIDS TO MEMORY

FOR THE CATECHISM.

ACTS OF FAITH, HOPE, CHARITY, AND CONTRITION.

ACT OF FAITH.

GREAT God! whatever through Thy Church
　　Thou teachest to be true,
I firmly do believe it all,
　　And shall confess it too.
Thou never canst deceived be,
　　Thou never canst deceive,
For Thou art truth itself, and Thou
　　Dost tell me to believe.
　　9*

ACT OF HOPE.

My God! I firmly hope in Thee,
  For Thou art great and good,
And gavest us Thine only Son
  To die upon the rood.
I hope through him for grace to live
  As Thy commandments teach,
And through Thy mercy when I die,
  The joys of heaven to reach.

ACT OF LOVE.

With all my heart, and soul, and strength,
  I love Thee, O my Lord,
For Thou art perfect, and all things
  Were made by Thy blest Word.
Like me to Thine own image made,
  My neighbor Thou didst make,
And as I love myself, I love
  My neighbor for Thy sake.

ACT OF CONTRITION.

Most holy God! my very soul
  With grief sincere is moved,
Because I have offended Thee,
  Whom I should e'er have loved.

Forgive me, Father! I am now,
Resolved to sin no more,
And by thy holy grace to shun
What made me sin before.

———— .

THE TEN COMMANDMENTS OF GOD.

I.

I AM thy God and Sovereign Lord,
Naught else must be as God adored.

II.

All sacred things thy reverence claim,
Take not in vain God's holy name.

III.

Keep holy every Sabbath-day,
And do not work, but rest and pray.

IV.

All honor to thy Parents pay, .
Nor their just wishes disobey.

V.

Treat all as kindly as you can,
Kill not, nor hate your fellow-man.

VI.

From lewd temptations turn with haste,
And never do an act unchaste.

VII.

Give what is due to every one,
And take not what is not thine own.

VIII.

Speak always what is true and fair,
Lie not, nor e'er false witness bear.

IX.

Preserve thy fancy free from stain,
And lustful thoughts ne'er entertain.

X.

Be just in purpose and design,
And covet not what is not thine.

THE SIX PRECEPTS OF THE CHURCH.

I.

Let not a Feast or Sunday pass
Without once hearing Holy Mass.

II.

Whene'er the Church shall so ordain,
Keep fast, or from flesh meat abstain.

III.

Make every twelvemonth once at least
A good Confession to your Priest.

IV.

Each year, at Easter time at least,
Approach the Eucharistic feast.

V.

The Priest must by the people live,
And you to him your mite should give.

VI.

The rules for Christian marriage made
Must be respected and obeyed.

———

GRACE.

GRACE is the light God gives the mind,
That we the truth may surely find—
Grace is the strength he gives free will,
His holy precepts to fulfill.

———

A SACRAMENT.

AN outward sign of inward grace
By Christ ordained and made—
A mystic rite by which his grace
Is to our souls conveyed.

THE SEVEN SACRAMENTS.

I.

WE are cleansed from sin original
  In Baptism's holy waters;
We are chosen heirs of heaven, and made
  God's happy sons and daughters.

II.

We are rendered perfect Christians when
  We are signed in Confirmation,
And God the Holy Ghost gives strength
  To conquer all temptation.

III.

Christ present in the Eucharist
  To worship we are bidden;
Beneath the forms of bread and wine
  The Lord is truly hidden.

IV.

All sins that after Baptism
  A man may have committed,
If he is sorry from his heart
  By Penance are remitted.

V.

The Last Anointing heals the flesh,
  New life and strength imparting;
Or else insures a happy death
  To souls from earth departing.

VI.

In Holy Order Priests receive
  Their heavenly commission,
With grace to worthily fulfill
  The duties of their mission.

VII.

In Matrimony, Christians are
  As man and wife united,
Receiving grace from God to keep
  The faith which they've plighted.

SEVEN CORPORAL WORKS OF MERCY.

Visit, give ransom, raiment, drink, and bread,
Shelter the homeless, and inter the dead.

SEVEN SPIRITUAL WORKS OF MERCY.

Teach, counsel, soothe, correct, forgive, and bear,
Think of the living and the dead in prayer.

THE SEVEN DEADLY SINS.

PRIDE is inordinate esteem that one
Has for himself, or what by him is done.*

Avarice is the immoderate love of gain
Which we have got, or which we would obtain.

Lust means all impure pleasure, be it sought
By look, by word, by action, or by thought.

Anger is passion quick and violent,
That moves the will some grievance to resent.

Gluttony is the abuse of drink and meat;
It does not eat to live, it lives to eat.

Envy's regret that others should do well,
As if their welfare 'gainst our own did tell.

Sloth is a cold disrelish that withdraws
The sluggish heart from God and from his laws.

THE EIGHT BEATITUDES.

BLESSED the poor in spirit, they are heirs
To wealth untold, for heaven itself is theirs.

----

*(Vanity means the inordinate desire
That other folks may praise us or admire.)

Blessed the meek, for without strife their hand
Shall be victorious, and possess the land.

Blessed are they that mourn, for God one day
Will comfort them, and wipe their tears away.

Blessed who hunger and who thirst, unskilled
In wiles, for justice, for they shall be filled.

Blessed the merciful, for they'll obtain
The mercy which they grant their fellow-men.

Blessed the clean of heart, for they shall see
The Lord in all his cloudless purity.

Blessed are the peace-makers kind and mild—
Children of God they shall be justly styled.

Blessed are they that suffer in the right,
For heaven's kingdom shall their cares requite.

CANTICLE ON THE BLESSED SACRA-MENT.

Hail! most holy Sacrament
Where God is our aliment.
In thee Jesus we behold—
His own tongue this truth has told.
10

In the Eucharistic bread,
With his flesh our souls are fed.
Who can doubt the word he spoke,
When that mystic bread he broke?

Man was lost in sin and shame—
To redeem him Jesus came;
Came the Father's equal Son,
Our frail nature to put on.

Son of man and Son of God,
O'er Judea's plains he trod.
Blessings round his footsteps fall—
Grace and truth he gives to all.

Came that ever-blessed night,
When, concealing all his might,
To be slaughtered by his foes
Like a helpless lamb he goes.

But before the fearful hour,
When was loosened hell's dark power,
He drew closer to his heart
Those with whom he had to part.

See! around the sacred board
Sit the twelve and their own Lord!
Who the flames of love can tell
That within his bosom dwell?

Hearken to his loving voice!
Hark! and let thy soul rejoice—
Pledged to thee as well as those
Is the gift he now bestows.

Ended is the obscure rite
Which belonged to Jewish night.
Shadowy figures now give way
To the splendor of new day.

Holding in his hands the bread,
"This my body is," he said;
"This the body, real, true,
I shall immolate for you."

Holding forth what now was wine,
"Take," he says, "this blood of mine—
Living blood which soon shall be
Shed, the world from sin to free.

Eat of this, my very flesh,
With my blood your souls refresh;
When my earthly course is run,
Do ye what I now have done."

'Twas the Word Divine that spoke!
He whose order could evoke
Out of nothing's dark abyss
All that was and all that is.

At his voice the glorious sun
First began his course to run.
He, too, summoned every star,
And all answered, " Here we are."

In the heavens and on the earth,
All things owe to him their birth.
He alone their being gave—
He can change, destroy, or save.

Ages come and ages go—
Age or change he cannot know.
And the word that spoke his will
Stands forever changeless still.

And the Apostles, ever true,
Did that which he bade them do—
Blessed the sacred bread and wine,
Changed to elements divine.

When before your vision pass
The dread mysteries of the Mass,
Jesus Christ is present still,
That same wonder to fulfill.

At the sacred Altar-stone
Stands the Priest, but not alone,
For the voice of God is heard
In the consecrating word.

Jesus did this promise make—
Made it for his mercy's sake;
And his word will faithful stay,
Never, never pass away.

Thus to flesh is changed the bread,
Wine into the blood he shed.
Lacketh he nor power nor will
What he promised to fulfill.

Heresy and fatal pride
May this mystery deride;
We faith's humble offering bring
To our Saviour and our King.

Jesus, who upon the cross
Saved us from eternal loss—
Jesus, living God on high,
In the Sacrament is nigh.

Adoration, honor, love,
Let us give to God above.
Chiefly let our praise be told
For the gift our altars hold.

[I am happy in being permitted to adorn my book with the foregoing admirable Canticle, composed by one of the most learned and distinguished ecclesiastics in America, and communicated to me by the author, to testify his approval of my exertions for the benefit of our children.]

10*

FOUR LAST THINGS TO BE REMEM-BERED.

PREPARE for Death—you'll surely die one day ;
But when, or where, or how, no man can say.

Fear Judgment—to a wise and mighty Lord
You must account for thought, and deed, and
    word.

Remember Hell to shun it—dark despair,
Fire, and the worm that never dies, are there.

Look up to Heaven !—if you are firm and true
In serving God, its joys are all for you.

THE SEVEN SORROWS OF THE B. V. M.

1.

By Simeon old the future's told
    Of God's incarnate Word,
And Mary's care is to prepare
    Her heart for sorrow's sword.

Mother ! our sins with seven swords
    Have pierced thy sacred breast,
But in thy presence and thy Lord's
    All sin we now detest.

2.

Rude soldiers stain fair Bethlehem's plain
    With children's rosy gore,
Warned from on high his parents fly
    With Christ to Egypt's shore.

                    Mother, &c.

3.

Through streets and ways Our Lady strays,
    Till three long days are done;
All sorrow past, she then at last
    Embraces her dear Son.

                    Mother, &c.

4.

Our Lady hears how Jesus bears
    His cross—oh, bitter load!
With heart resigned she hastes to find
    And meet him on the road.

                    Mother, &c.

5.

Mount Calvary's brow is gained, and now
    The Lord they crucify;
While to fulfill the Almighty's will
    His mother stands near by.

                    Mother, &c.

6.

With pious care his friends repair
To take the body down ;
In death He sleeps, his mother weeps,
And shares his thorny crown.

Mother, &c.

7.

They reach the cave, and in its grave
The Saviour's body lies ;
His mother's grief finds no relief
Till from the dead He rise.

Mother, &c.

ASPIRATION.

A SPIRIT sent by Satan, Mother,
Tempts me to go astray—
Send one of thy good angels, Mother,
To drive him far away.

THE FOURTEEN STATIONS OF THE CROSS.

I.

THE Son of God came down from heaven,
Upon the earth to dwell,
And man condemns to cruel death
The heart that loved him well.

Thou goest forth, O Blessed Lord,
  To suffer death for me,
And I too wish for thee to live—
  I wish to die for thee.

II.

He taketh up his heavy Cross,
  And bears the crushing load;
And as he meekly journeys on,
  His blood bedews the road.

Thou goest forth, &c.

III.

Rude soldiers press and goad him on,
  And straiten him around,
And now, beneath his weighty Cross,
  He falls upon the ground.

Thou goest forth, &c.

IV.

His Mother hastens forth to join
  The Son she loved so well;
Their glances meet, their hearts are filled
  With grief no tongue can tell.

Thou goest forth, &c.

V.

They fear the Saviour may expire
   Beneath his heavy load,
And Simon is compelled to bear
   His Cross along the road.

            Thou goest forth, &c.

VI.

A Jewish woman wipes his face—
   Her pity to reward,
Upon her veil remains impressed
   An image of the Lord.

            Thou goest forth, &c.

VII.

The Saviour falls a second time,
   Oppressed with bitter pain ;
The soldiers force him to arise,
   And journey on again.

            Thou goest forth, &c.

VIII.

The Daughters of Jerusalem
   Bewail his cruel fate;
He bids them for their children weep,
   Before it is too late.

            Thou goest forth, &c.

IX.

He's urged to move with quicker step;
  His blood in torrents flows;
Again, again he falls to earth,
  Beneath their cruel blows.

> Thou goest forth, &c.

X.

The soldiers strip with violence
  The garments from his flesh,
And every wound he had received
  Is made to bleed afresh.

> Thou goest forth, &c.

XI.

They lay him down upon the Cross;
  They nail his hands and feet;
The Cross is raised, and he is left
  His coming death to meet.

> Thou goest forth, &c.

XII.

Three hours of agony had passed
  Since he was crucified;
His work was done, his hour was come—
  He bowed his head and died.

> Thou goest forth, &c.

XIII.

Now his disciples come and take
  The body from the Cross;
His Mother folds it in her arms,
  And mourns her bitter loss.

      Thou goest forth, &c.

XIV.

His followers bear him to the tomb,
  Prepared with pious care,
Then silently depart, and leave
  The sacred body there.

      Thou goest forth, &c.

THE END.

INTRODUCTORY REMARKS,

BY

SIGNOR SPERANZA.

———

WHEN I had the honor of being chosen by the Rev. Dr. Cummings to work with him in preparing this collection for the public, I found myself limited in composition to short musical phrases, and a very brief compass of notes, the melodies being intended for children. Children, even in large numbers, and entirely ignorant of music, will easily acquire them. The method I would recommend for teaching them is the *echo* system. It is practised in the following manner:

The teacher sings one phrase himself, then, with a tap er little stroke of a ruler, gives the signal that the children are to repeat immediately the phrase he has sung. If they make any mistake, the teacher will repeat the phrase until they learn it well. One phrase being learned, the next will be taken up, the teacher singing and the children following immediately at the signal as before, until phrases enough are learned to form a period. The teacher will go over the phrases already learned, and the children will repeat first two phrases at a time, and then four, until the whole period is learned. One period being learned, the others will follow, until the whole piece is sung correctly.

11

To obtain good results from this method, the following rules must be carefully observed:

1. Strict discipline must be maintained among the scholars.

2. The person teaching must sing with a distinct, decided, and clean enunciation of both notes and words, bringing out more expressly those notes which the scholars seem to have most difficulty in seizing with precision.

3. The children must be trained and compelled to sing always *sotto-voce*, until they have learned well the piece they are studying.

4. It is of the greatest importance that the scholars shall not begin to sing until the signal is given by a tap of the ruler, when they must begin immediately, and all together.

The habit of singing very piano while learning has an excellent effect on children, who are so organized that it is with the greatest difficulty they can be induced to pass into the upper register, or the *voce di testa*. If they are called upon to sing an ascending scale, they keep on as long as the lower range, the *voce di petto*, and *voce di mezzo* will allow, but when they get up to the high notes they either stop, or else force the voice to a scream. To allow them to go on in this way would put them out of breath, and might do them serious injury, ruining their voices perhaps forever.

In recommending the use of the echo system, I speak from experience of its good results, obtained in the public singing-schools of Turin, and especially in the orphan asylum of that city, known as La Generala, where I had under my direction as many as sixteen hundred children

at the same time. By means of this system they learned
to execute not only songs in one voice, but even masses,
etc., in two voices, which they sang in the chapel of the
institution on great festivals. In six months they improved so far as to possess quite an extensive repertoire
of sacred music.

DOMENICO SPERANZA.

The only airs in the collection not composed by Signor
Speranza are Nos. 10 and 11, which, as they have had
the luck to become quite popular with the new words,
we have left unchanged; 22 and 23, two favorite sacred
choruses by Verdi; and 62, which is an old ecclesiastical
melody selected for the canticle on the Blessed Eucharist
by its author. This canticle is the only piece in the book
the words of which were not written by Rev. Dr. Cummings.

N. B.—Where a song is set to more than one voice, the
first part alone may be sung, if necessary, by all.

Songs for Catholic Schools.

No. 1.

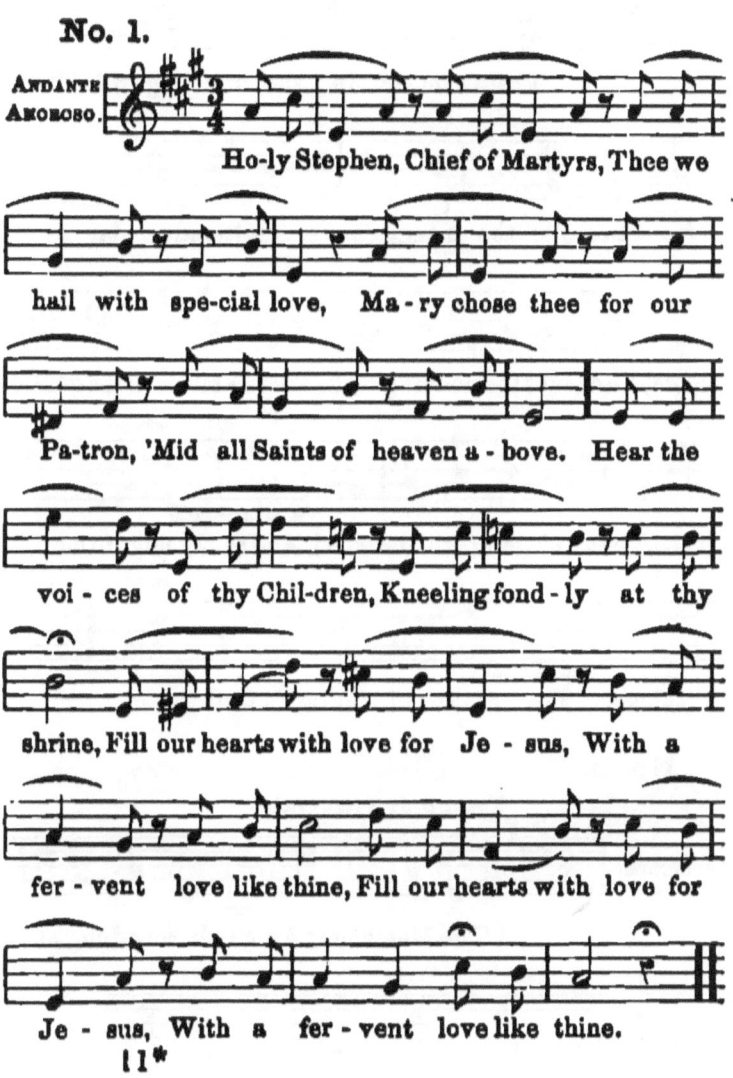

ANDANTE AMOROSO.

Ho-ly Stephen, Chief of Martyrs, Thee we

hail with spe-cial love, Ma - ry chose thee for our

Pa-tron, 'Mid all Saints of heaven a - bove. Hear the

voi - ces of thy Chil-dren, Kneeling fond - ly at thy

shrine, Fill our hearts with love for Je - sus, With a

fer - vent love like thine, Fill our hearts with love for

Je - sus, With a fer - vent love like thine.

11*

No. 2.

ANDANTINO GRAZIOSO.

There's music in the bubbling rill, That

fro - lics o'er the mead, That makes the silver dai - sy

bloom, And laves the nodding reed. There's music in the gentle

a piacere.

breeze, That whispers thro' the wood, And softly sings to mortal

Grandioso.

things,   The praise of   nature's God.

No. 3.

Tempo di Pastorale.

AFFETTUOSO.

The Messenger An-gel de-scend-ing at

night, Chased si - lence and sha-dow with mu - sic and

light, The shepherds of Beth-le-hem heard on the

plain, The Mes-sen-ger An-gel, and this was his

una voce sola.
strain: "May peace be to mor-tals and glo-ry to

heaven, The Pro-mised of old to man-kind has been

given, Re-joice at the splendor that heralds his

birth, The Sa-viour, the Sa-viour has come up-on

tutti con gioja.
earth, The Saviour, the Saviour has come up-on earth."

No. 4.

ANDANTE
GRANDIOSO.

The earth, O Lord, re-joi-ces, And

sings with glad acclaim A hymn of ma - ny voi-ces, In

hon-or of thy name. We join the hap - py chorus, That

hails the morning light, And bless the Lord that o'er us Kept

mancando.

lov-ing watch all night, all night, all night.

No. 5.

ANDANTINO
AMOROSO.

Hail Vir - gin of virgins, Thy praises we

sing, Thy throne is in heaven, Thy Son is its King.

The saints and the an-gels, Thy glo-ry pro-claim, All

na - tions de - vout - ly   Bow down at   thy name.

No. 6.

ANDANTE
MAESTOSO.

God of glo-ry, God   of might, Foe of

er - ror, Friend of   right.   Roll the tem - pest

Far   a - way, Smile in sunbeams While we pray.

No. 7.

GRANDIOSO.

World   of Grace! mys-ter-ious   Temple!

Ho - ly,   a - pos - to - lic, One! Nev - er   chang-ing,

ev - er   bless - ing, Ev' - ry   age and ev' - ry

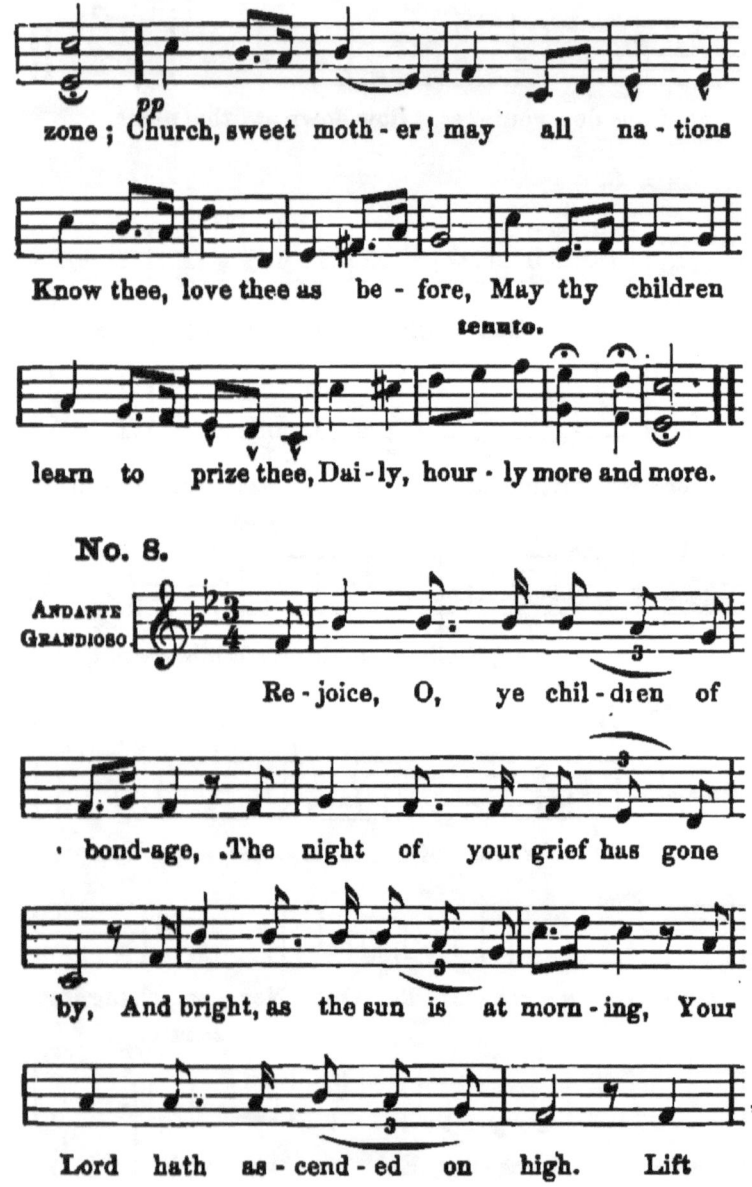

zone ; Church, sweet moth - er ! may   all   na - tions

Know thee, love thee as   be - fore, May thy   children

learn to   prize thee, Dai - ly, hour - ly more and more.

No. 8.

Re - joice,   O,   ye chil - dren of

• bond-age, .The night of   your grief has gone

by, And bright, as   the sun is   at morn - ing, Your

Lord   hath   as - cend - ed   on   high.   Lift

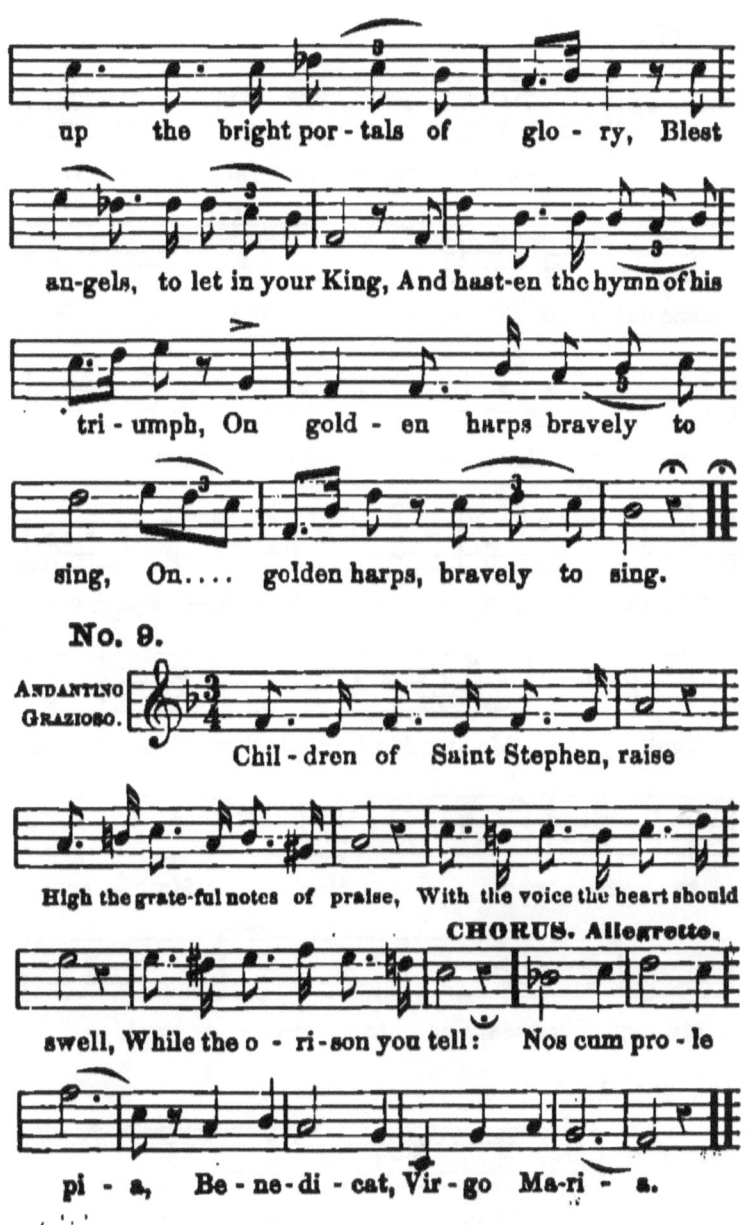

up   the   bright por - tals of   glo - ry, Blest

an-gels, to let in your King, And hast-en the hymn of his

tri - umph, On   gold - en   harps bravely to

sing,   On.... golden harps, bravely to sing.

No. 9.

ANDANTINO
GRAZIOSO.

Chil - dren of   Saint Stephen, raise

High the grate-ful notes of praise, With the voice the heart should

CHORUS. Allegretto.

swell, While the o - ri - son you tell: Nos cum pro - le

pi - a,   Be - ne - di - cat, Vir - go Ma-ri - a.

No. 10.

GRAZIOSO.

Oh, Ma - ry, Moth-er Ma - ry! We
place our trust in thee— Our faith shall nev - er
va - ry, Though weak the flesh may be ;
Too oft with steps un - wa - ry, From du - ty's path we've
bent,   Oh, Ma - ry, Moth-er Ma - ry, Thou teach us
to   re - pent,   Oh, Ma - ry, Moth - er
Ma - ry, Thou teach us   to   re - - pent.

No. 11.

ANDANTINO.

When our Saviour wished to prove, All the

full - ness of his love, He gave us ere life was

Stringendo.

spent The thrice Ho - ly Sa - cra - ment. It is

Ritard.

here his burning heart Would to all its flames im

ten. ꞏ  a tempo. 3

- part; Thus He speaks with love di - vine,

Give me, Oh, give me that heart of thine,

Give me, oh give me that heart of thine.

No. 12.

ANDANTINO
AMOROSO.

In highest heaven where stands the throne Of

12

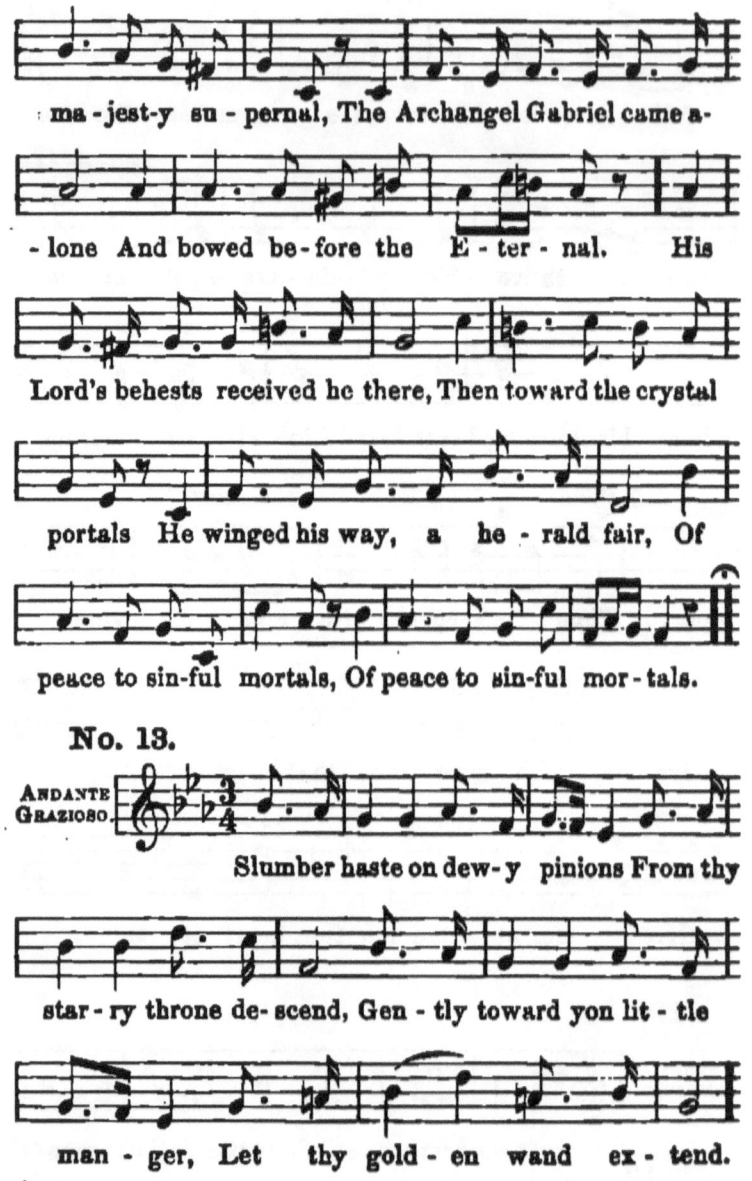

ma - jest-y su - pernal, The Archangel Gabriel came a-

- lone And bowed be - fore the E - ter - nal. His

Lord's behests received he there, Then toward the crystal

portals He winged his way, a he - rald fair, Of

peace to sin-ful mortals, Of peace to sin-ful mor - tals.

No. 13.

ANDANTE
GRAZIOSO.

Slumber haste on dew - y pinions From thy

star - ry throne de - scend, Gen - tly toward yon lit - tle

man - ger, Let thy gold - en wand ex - tend.

On his moth-er's bo - som slow - ly, Lo! the

Babe re - clines his head; Sweet-ly o'er his wea - ried

sen - ses Balm - y sleep its charm hath spread.

No. 14.

CHORUS.

MAESTOSO.

Star of the o - cean, 'Mid life's com-

- mo - tion We with de - vo - tion Fol - low thy light;

Keep us still wa - ry, Lest we may va - ry,

FINE. SOLO.

Lento.

Ma - ry, sweet Ma - ry, Guide us a - right. O,

spotless Queen of Virgins, With shining lilies crowned, Grant

CHORUS.

we thy youthful daughters, May pure like thee be found.

No. 15.

AFFETTUOSO.

From thy bright throne a - bove the

sky, Look down on us, O Moth - er

sweet, And smile up - on the gift which I Here

of - fer, kneel - ing at thy feet. O!

Moth - er of my God and mine, I've

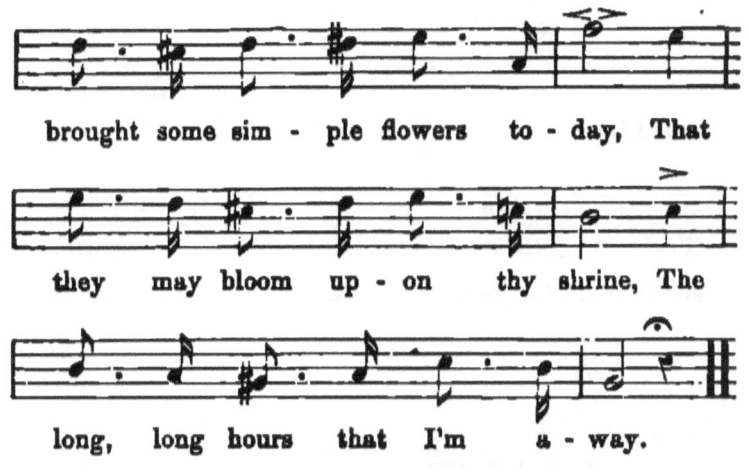

brought some sim - ple flowers to - day, That

they may bloom up - on thy shrine, The

long, long hours that I'm a - way.

No. 16.

ANDANTINO AMOROSO.

The Tear of In - no - cence how

bright It gush - es from the eye, It wins the

sym - pa - thy of men, The blessings of the

sky. Be - fore the ten - der in - fant's tongue Has

12*

learned to   shape   a   sound,   It   tells   with

sim - ple e - lo-quence His lit - tle wants a - round.

No. 17.

ANDANTE
SOSTENUTO.

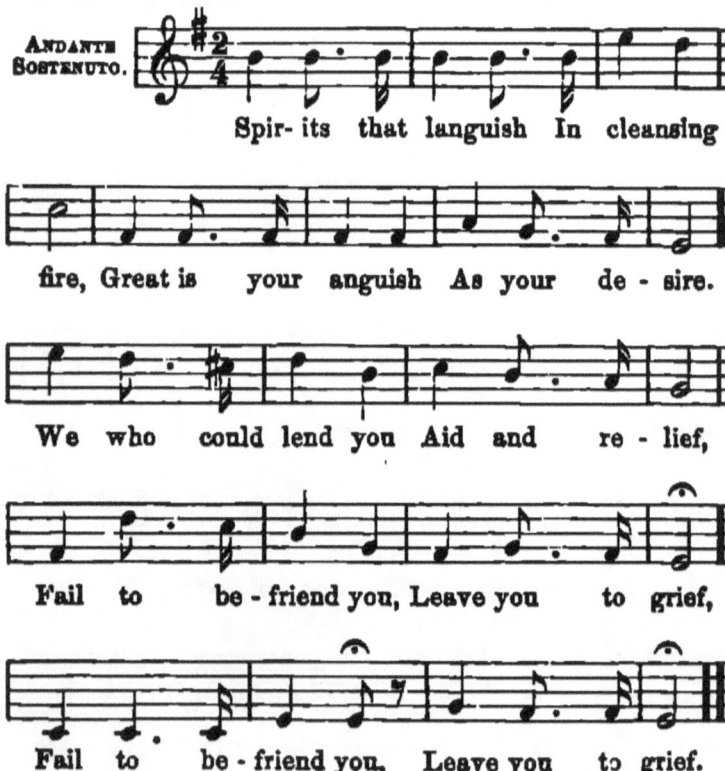

Spir- its that languish In cleansing

fire, Great is   your anguish As your   de - sire.

We   who   could lend you Aid and   re - lief,

Fail   to   be - friend you, Leave you   to grief,

Fail   to   be - friend you,   Leave you   to grief.

No. 18.

Great God, I call up-on thy name And

bow be-fore thy throne, A - mid the si - lent shades of

night, Unwatched, unseen, a - lone. How oft a -

- midst the glare of day, When pleasure's throng was

nigh, I have for - got - ten that I

moved, Be - neath thy watch - ful eye.

No. 19.

Tempo di Marcia.

Ere Peace and Freedom hand in

hand Went forth to bless this hap-py land, And

make it their a - - bode. It was the foot- stool

of a throne, But now no scep - tre

here is known, No king is feared but

God, No king is feared but God.

No. 20.

MAESTOSO.

Thy power, O Lord, is bound-less

power, Thy love is bound - less love, And

for that love and by that power Thou

CHORUS.

com - est from a - bove. Son of God we

bow be - fore thee, Bless - - ed

Lento molto.

Sa - viour, we a - dore.... thee.

No. 2L

ANDANTINO
AMOROSO.

How kind it is of you to come, Bright

An - gel from your star-ry home, And watch by night and

watch by day Be - side a sin - ful child of clay.

How good and pure I ought to be Who

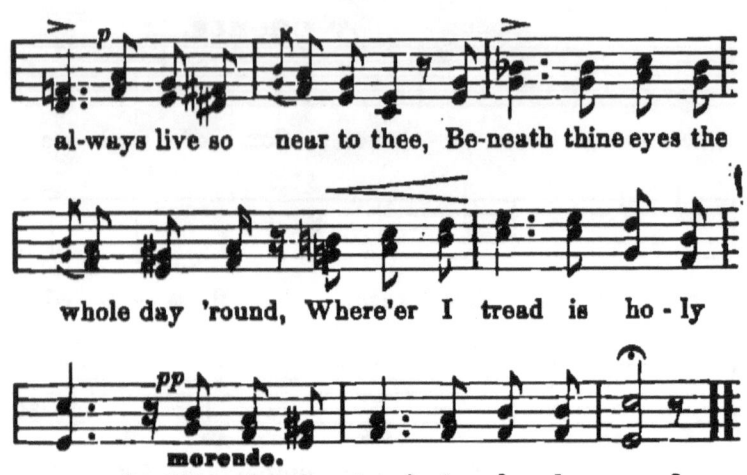

al-ways live so near to thee, Be-neath thine eyes the

whole day 'round, Where'er I tread is ho - ly

ground, Where'er I tread is ho - ly ground.

No. 22 and 24.

Haste, fond Mem'ry, thy vi - gor re-
Soul a - wak-en, in sad-ness why

- call - ing, Haste a - way to the val - leys and
lan - guish, Break a - way from thy fears and thy

mountains, Where the breeze o'er Ju - dea's bright
fet - ters, Feel the cour-age that rouses and

foun - tains, Cools the air... of our dear na - tive
bet = *ters, Leave the des - ert, its sad - ness and*

land, Hov - er fond - ly o'er Jor - dan's clear
gloom. Look a - broad, hon - est work has its

wa - ters, Mark the tur - rets of Si - on now
beau - ty, Earn - est hearts can for - get... their own

fall - ing; O! Ju - de - a, thy sons and thy
an - guish, And can toil in the vine-yard of

daugh - ters, Weep for thee.. on this bar - bar-ous
du ' - ty, While the slug - gard sits wail - ing his

. strand. Harp of Gold! hast thou part - ed with
doom. Sad - dest hearts 'neath their ash - es have

Glo - - ry, That thou hang-est un-strung on the
em - - bers, That will glow if we do good to

wil - low ? O ! as bil-'low rolls on af - ter
oth - ers, For the prayers of our nee - di - er

bil - low, Let the mu - sic rush o'er thy bright
broth - ers, Turn to bless - ings and fol - low us

chords. Dark and sad, like poor So - ly - ma's
home. We are all of one bo - dy the

sto - ry, Breathe a dirge mixed with deep sighs of
members, Here to - day be we shar - ers in

sor - row, Or from mem-'ry some bright dit - ty
sor - row, For we hope to be shar-ers to

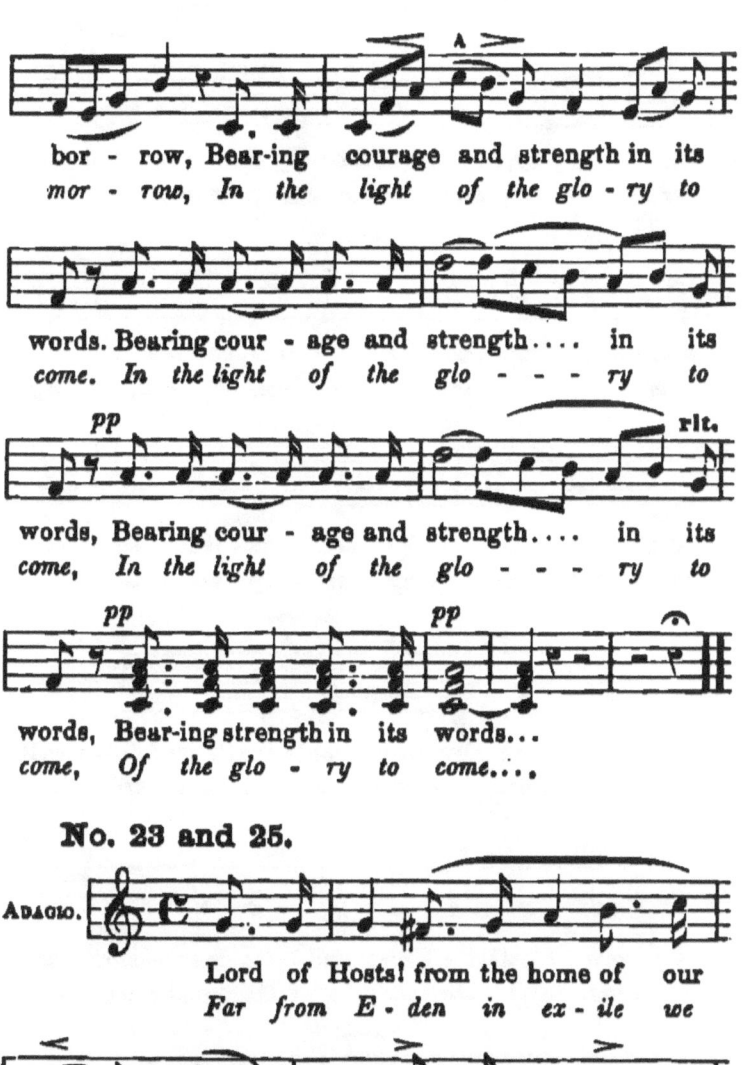

bor - row, Bear-ing courage and strength in its
mor - row, In the light of the glo - ry to

words. Bearing cour - age and strength.... in its
come. In the light of the glo - - - ry to

words, Bearing cour - age and strength.... in its
come, In the light of the glo - - - ry to

words, Bear-ing strength in its words...
come, Of the glo - ry to come....

No. 23 and 25.

ADAGIO.

Lord of Hosts! from the home of our
Far from E - den in ex - ile we

childhood Thou hast called us with prom - is - es
wan - der, 'Mid the deep gloom of night and of

13

ho - - - ly, We march'd boldly thro' waste and thro'
er - - - ror, And of dreams we grow fond - er and

wild - wood, Sure to con - - quer, yet rea - dy to
fond - er, If we call not, O Lord, on thy

die. But our looks are de - ject - ed and
power. While we pray ev' - ry vis - ion of

low - ly, And thy ser - vants are bowed down with
ter - ror Melts a - way like the dew - drops at

sor - row; Shall the Cross and its war - riors to -
morn-ing, And the wiles of the proud tempt - er

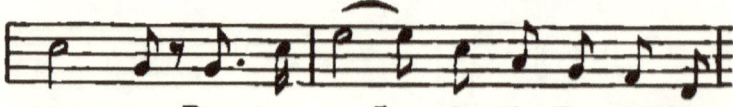

- mor - row, Prove a scoff when the Pay-nim draw
scorn - ing, We are free.. as in E - den's lost

nigh? We   re - mem - ber...... dear Lombar - dy's
lower.   O,   this world when.... it scat - ters its

moun - tains, Her...... vineyards, her fields rich in
flow - ers, When it gath - ers its tro - phies a -

glo - ry, Her fresh breez - es,.... her mur - mur - ing
- round me, May be - guile for.... a few fleet - ing

foun - tains, The green bow - ers that wave in her
hours,.... · But my heart must be wretch - ed, or

land. Ah! fond mem - 'ry, thou'rt scarce - ly a
thine. Then be - fore Death has spread his dark

bless - ing, Thou re - call - est our childhood's sweet
pin - ion, And the spell of its sha - dow has

sto - ry,   But we're roused from thy dream - y   ca -
bound me,   Let   me bow   to   my Sa - viour's do -

- ress - ing,   By   the   glow   of   the hot des - ert
- *min - ion;   Let   his   glo - ry   or Cross still   be*

sand,   By   the glow......   of   the
mine,   Let   his   glo - ry,   or Cross

hot   sand,   the   hot   de - sert
be   mine,   or   Cross   still   be

sand,   the hot   des - ert   sand......
mine,   or Cross   still   be   mine......

No. 26.

SOLO.

Andante Sostenuto.

Almighty Sire! I'm dust, Unbounded

power is thine, Weak-ness and want are mine;

CHORUS.

In thee my love, my trust. Sanc-tus,..

Maestoso.

.... Sanc-tus De - us,... Sanc-tus,.. Sanc-tus

Piu lento.

for - tis,.... Sanc - - tus Im - - mor -

-ta - - lis, Mi - se - re - re no - bis.

No. 27.

ANDANTE AFFETTUOSO.

God, the Ho - ly Ghost, Life - giv - er,

Of the three blest persons third, Humbly kneeling we a-

13*

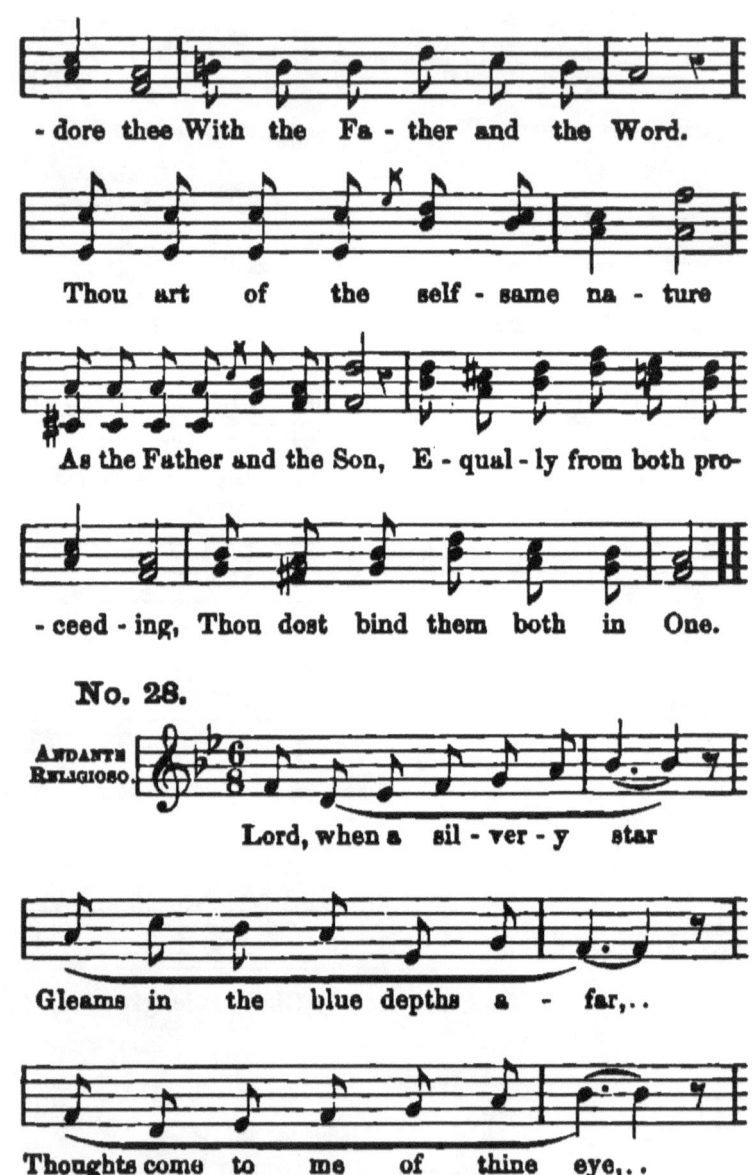

- dore thee With the Fa - ther and the Word.

Thou art of the self - same na - ture

As the Father and the Son, E - qual - ly from both pro-

- ceed - ing, Thou dost bind them both in One.

No. 28.

ANDANTE
RELIGIOSO.

Lord, when a sil - ver - y star

Gleams in the blue depths a - far,..

Thoughts come to me of thine eye,..

Look - ing on us from the sky...

Lord, when a trem - u lous beam

Sleeps on the sha - dow - y stream,

Thoughts come to me of thy love,

Brightening our hearts from a - bove.

No. 29.

ANDANTINO GRAZIOSO.

O brightness of e - ter - nal

light, I wor - ship at thy feet Though all un -

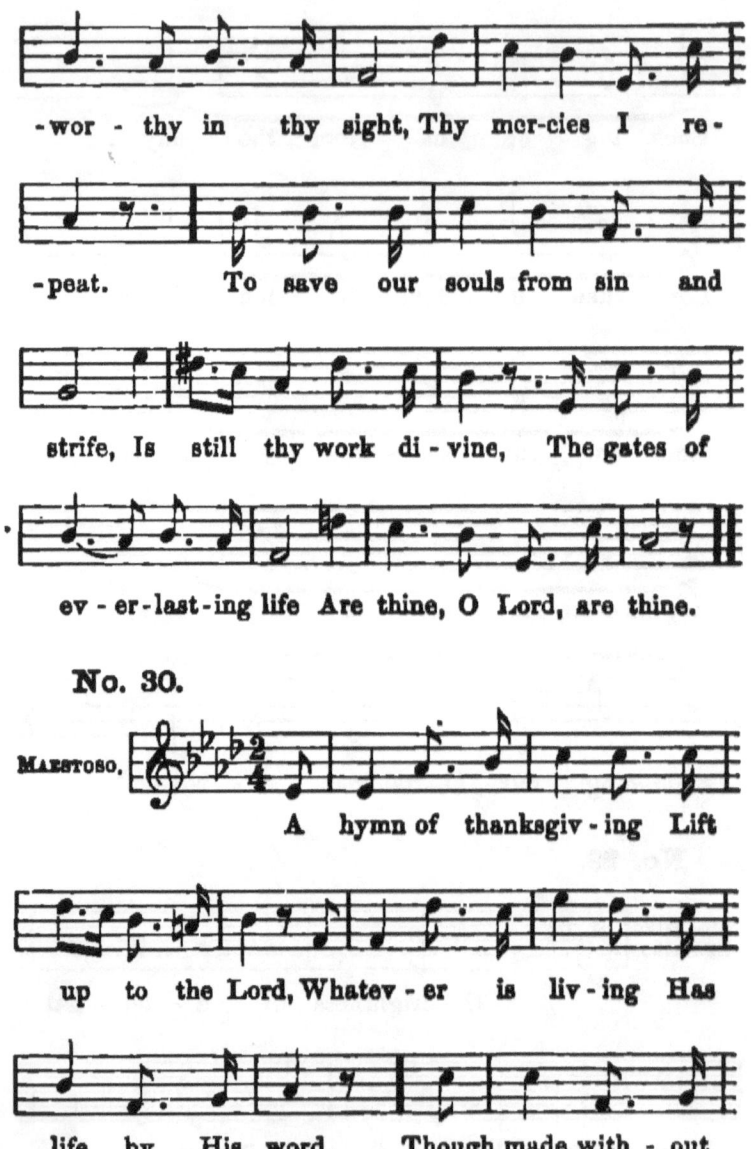

-wor - thy in thy sight, Thy mer-cies I re -

-peat.   To save our souls from sin and

strife, Is still thy work di - vine, The gates of

ev - er - last - ing life Are thine, O Lord, are thine.

No. 30.

MAESTOSO.

A hymn of thanksgiv - ing Lift

up to the Lord, Whatev - er is liv - ing Has

life by His word.   Though made with - out

merit By mer-cy a-lone, Our soul is a

spir-it, Re-sem-bling his own, Our

soul is a spir-it, Re-sembling his own.

No. 31.

Andante Maestoso.

When the air is warm and bright

Think of God who made the light. If the

tem-pest Should draw nigh: Chil-dren fear not,

'Twill go by, Chil-dren fear not, 'Twill go by.

No. 32.

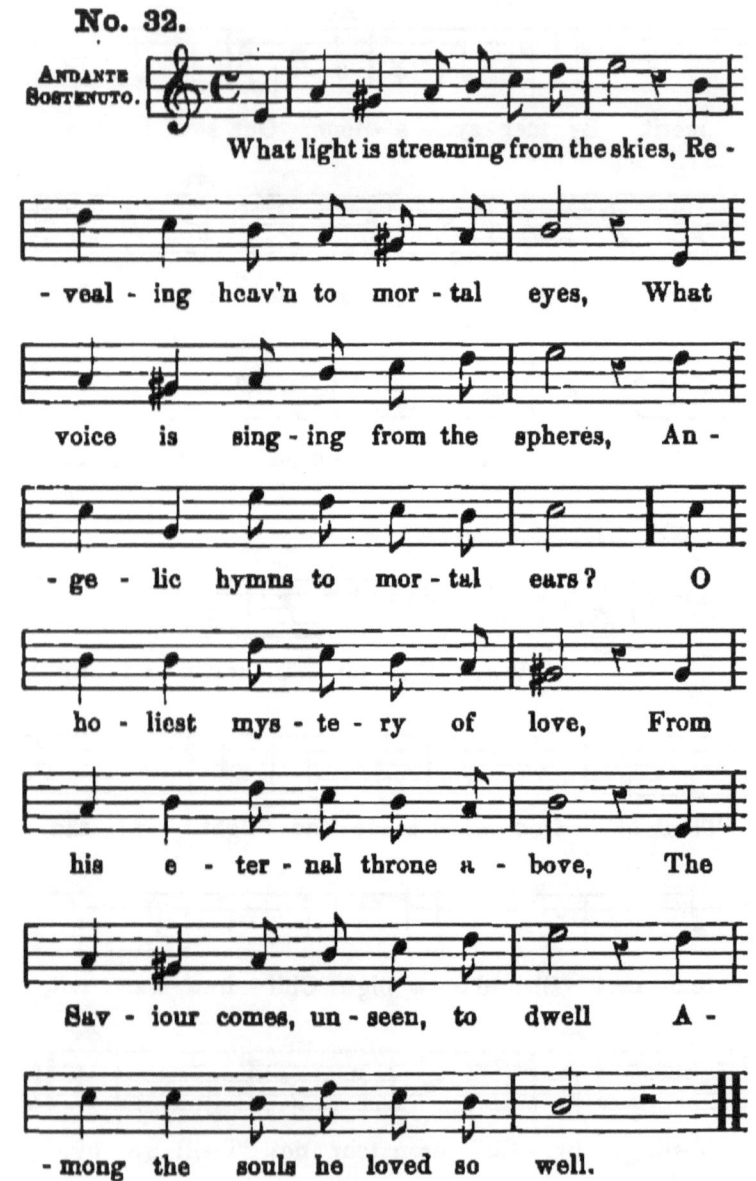

Andante Sostenuto.

What light is streaming from the skies, Re-
-veal - ing heav'n to mor - tal eyes, What
voice is sing - ing from the spheres, An -
- ge - lic hymns to mor - tal ears? O
ho - liest mys - te - ry of love, From
his e - ter - nal throne a - bove, The
Sav - iour comes, un - seen, to dwell A -
- mong the souls he loved so well.

No. 33.

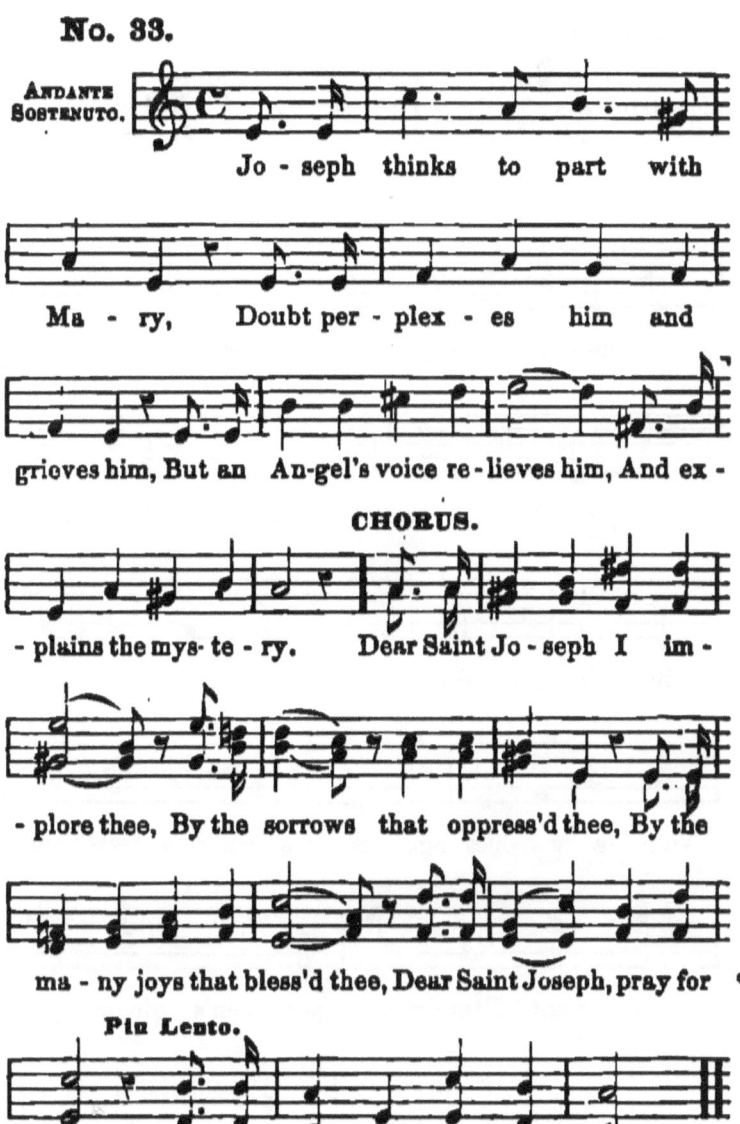

Jo - seph thinks to part with Ma - ry, Doubt per - plex - es him and grieves him, But an An-gel's voice re - lieves him, And ex - plains the mys- te - ry.

CHORUS.

Dear Saint Jo - seph I im - plore thee, By the sorrows that oppress'd thee, By the ma - ny joys that bless'd thee, Dear Saint Joseph, pray for me,

Piu Lento.

Dear Saint Jo - seph, pray for me.

No. 34.

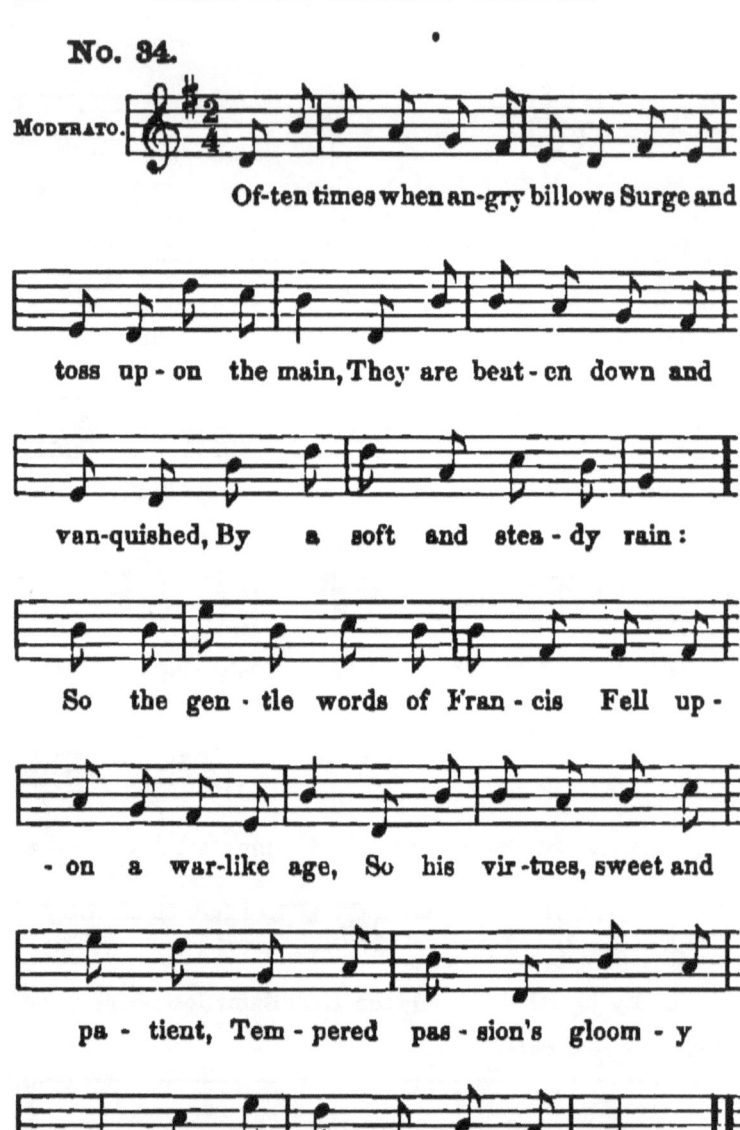

MODERATO.

Of-ten times when an-gry billows Surge and

toss up-on the main, They are beat-en down and

van-quished, By a soft and stea-dy rain:

So the gen-tle words of Fran-cis Fell up-

-on a war-like age, So his vir-tues, sweet and

pa-tient, Tem-pered pas-sion's gloom-y

rage, Tem-pered pas-sion's gloom-y rage.

No. 35.

Jane de Chan - tal, wor - thy
pu - pil Of the great and good De Sales, Thee our
song with pi - ous hom-age, On this fes - tal morn-ing
hails. Nurtured in thy father's ca - stle, When a
sweet and gen-tle girl, Thou wert nev - er spoiled by
gran - deur, Nor by fash - ion's gid - dy
whirl, Nor by Fash - ion's gid - dy whirl.

14

No. 36.

MAESTOSO.

A hymn to Saint Vincent de Paul, The
A - postle of broth - er - ly love, He
cared for the great and the small, As
sons of one Fa - ther a - bove. He
taught men in lu - xu - ry's dome The
wis - dom that fear - eth the Lord, He
taught men in pov - er - ty's home, The
pa - tience that trusts in his word.

No. 37.

Concitato.

O Mag-da-len, O Mag-da-len, I
see thee in the sup-per-hall, I
hear the sob thou gav-est then, I
see the tear-drop gush and fall. A
sor-row some-thing like thy own, Is
bu-sy in my sin-ful heart, But
while I sigh and while I moan, I
feel I am not what thou art.

No. 38.

MAESTOSO.

Vir - gin daughter of Cas-tile, All thy

coun-try's old - en worth, All her knightly fire and

zeal Burned with - in thee from thy birth.

Ah ! the world with cun - ning art   Strove its

i - dols to   en-throne, In the warm and no - ble

heart, God had formed to   be   his own,

No. 39.

ANDANTE
MAESTOSO.

Help of Chris - tians   while   the

com - bat Deep - ens round us, we be -

- seech thee, Let our pray'r - ful voi - ces

reach thee, Give as - sist - ance, ere we fall.

Life on earth is cease-less war - fare, Ma - ny

fears and cares dis-tress us, Ma-ny are the foes that

press us, But thou't save us from them all.

No. 40.

Una voce Sola.

ANDANTINO
GRAZIOSO.

Snow and rain have van - ished,

14*

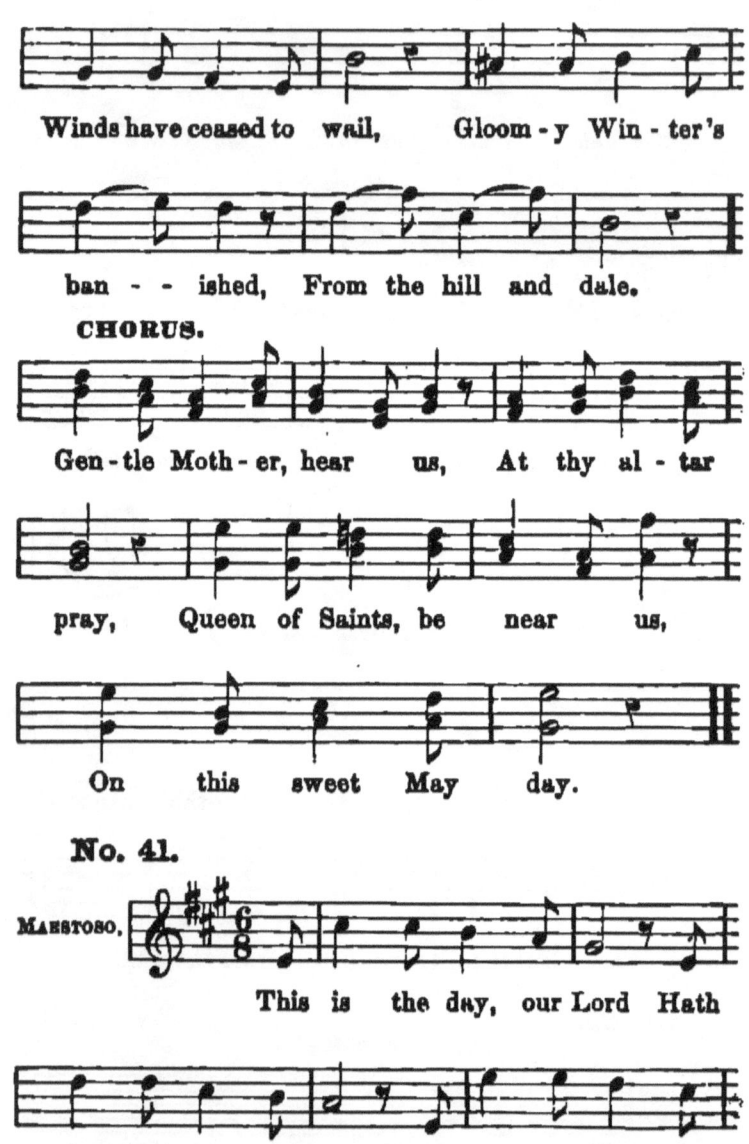

Winds have ceased to wail, Gloom - y Win - ter 's

ban - - ished, From the hill and dale.

CHORUS.

Gen - tle Moth - er, hear us, At thy al - tar

pray, Queen of Saints, be near us,

On this sweet May day.

No. 41.

MAESTOSO.

This is the day, our Lord Hath

cho - sen for his own, Come, mor - tals from your

toil,   And wor - ship at   his   throne.   Lift

up   your hearts in prayer,   And let your wants be

known. This   is   the   day,   our   Lord   Hath

cho - sen for   his own,   This   is   the day,   our

Lord   Hath cho - sen   for   his   own.

No. 42.

Andante Affettuoso.

At night the wealth-y   cit - i -

- zen,   Had turned   him from   the   door,   The

on - ly friends a - round him were   The

low - - ly   and   the   poor.   Yet

to   his   Fa - ther's will   re - signed,   The

new - - born   in - - fant   smiled ;   This

came   to   pass   in   Beth - le - hem,   When

Je - - sus   was   a   child,

No. 43.

ANDANTE
MAESTOSO.

There are sev - en bright spir - its that

stand, Near the throne of Je - ho - vah in

heaven, And to these sev - en Spir - its com -

- mand O - ver all the good An - gels is

given; They keep watch 'neath a ban - ner of

light, Up - on God's ho - ly moun - tain un -

- rolled; They are clad in full ar - mor so

bright That it flash - es like jew - els and gold.

No. 44.

ANDANTE AFFETUOSO.

Most Ho - ly Trin - i - ty, One
God, Im - mense in maj - es - ty, All power in
heaven and earth is thine, All things be - long to
thee. *Una sola voce.* I of - fer up the Ho - ly Mass This
morn - ing with the aim Of bless-ing *CHORUS.*
thy al - mighty power, And worship - ing thy name.

No. 45.

ANDANTE SOSTENUTO.

God of mer - cy, hear thy

peo - ple, While they hum - bly pray be -

- fore thee ; By thy good - ness we .im -

- plore thee, Save, O Lord, the Com - mon -

Uua Solo voce.

- wealth. Bless the land with peace and

plen - ty ; Keep in broth - er - ly com -

CHORUS.

- mun - ion, All the States of all the

Piu grandiose.

Un - ion, Save, O Lord, the Commonwealth.

No. 46.

I hear a voice from Beth-lehem, The

moan of winds re - sem -bling, It swell - eth up-ward

fit - ful - ly, Then fall - eth weak - ly trem-bling.

'Tis Ra - chel, mourn-ing bit - ter - ly, Her

young in cold death sleep-ing, O'er Ra - ma spreadeth

drear-i - ly, The cho - rus of her weep-ing,

No. 47.

Hear the word Of the Lord,

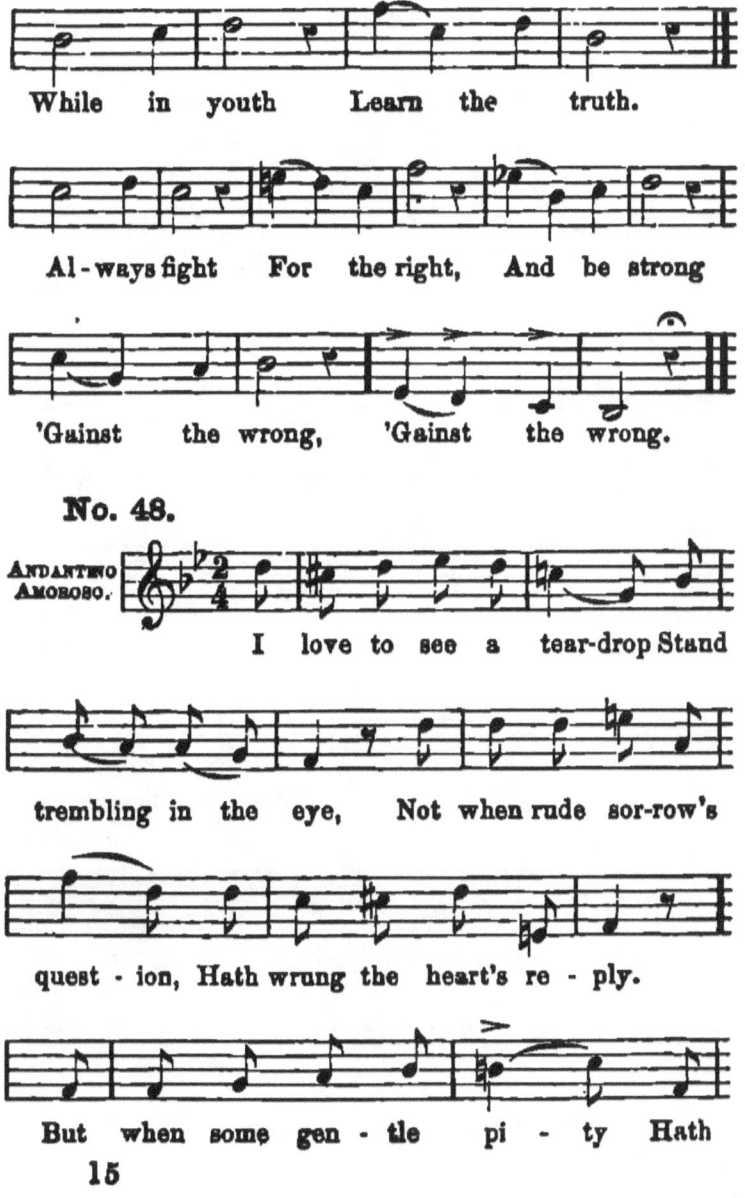

While in youth Learn the truth.

Al-ways fight For the right, And be strong

'Gainst the wrong, 'Gainst the wrong.

No. 48.

ANDANTINO AMOROSO.

I love to see a tear-drop Stand

trembling in the eye, Not when rude sor-row's

quest - ion, Hath wrung the heart's re - ply.

But when some gen - tle pi - ty Hath

15

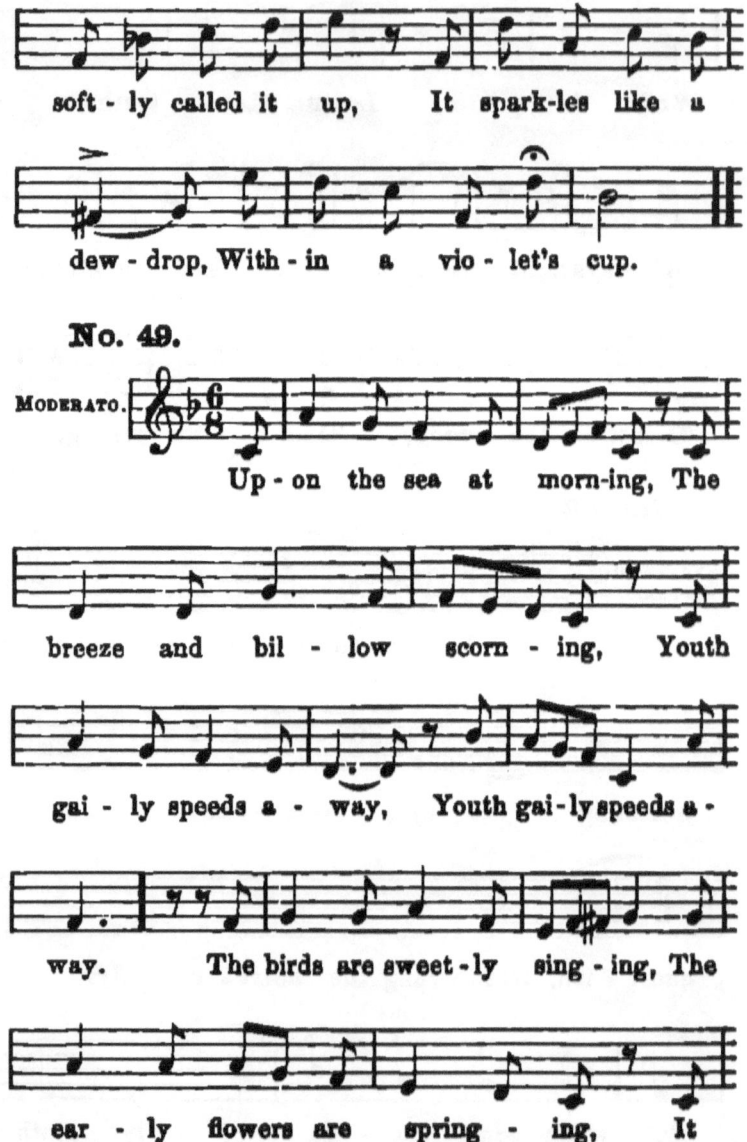

soft - ly called it up, It spark-les like a

dew - drop, With - in a vio - let's cup.

No. 49.

MODERATO.

Up - on the sea at morn-ing, The

breeze and bil - low scorn - ing, Youth

gai - ly speeds a - way, Youth gai-ly speeds a -

way. The birds are sweet - ly sing - ing, The

ear - ly flowers are spring - ing, It

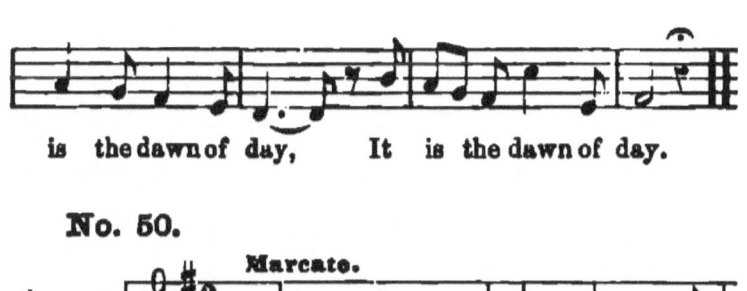

is the dawn of day, It is the dawn of day.

No. 50.

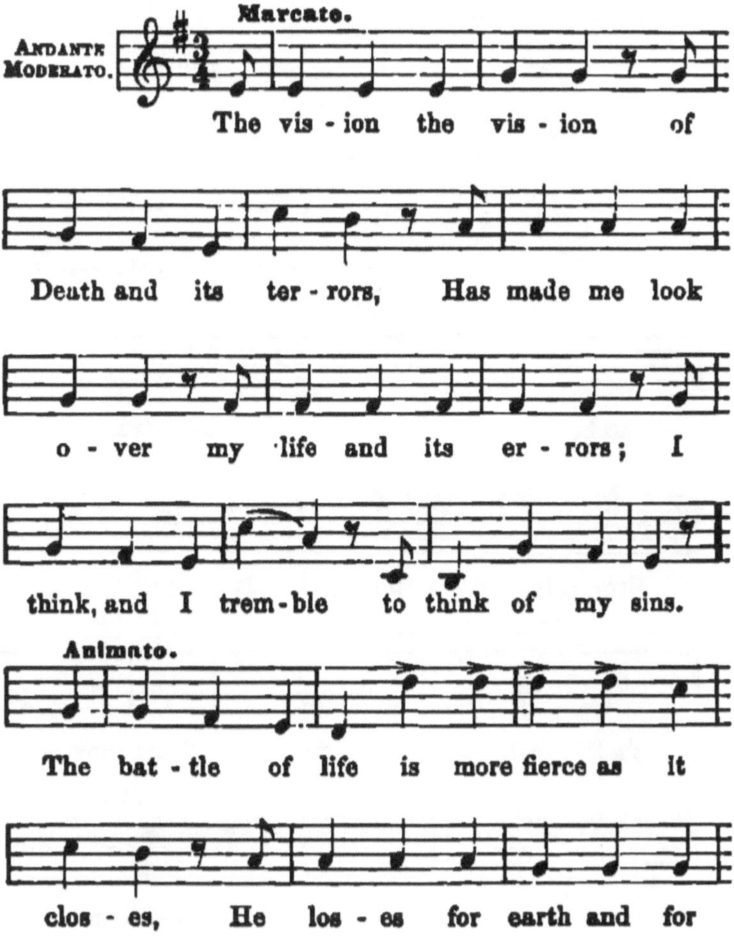

The vis - ion the vis - ion of

Death and its ter - rors, Has made me look

o - ver my life and its er - rors; I

think, and I trem - ble to think of my sins.

Animato.

The bat - tle of life is more fierce as it

clos - es, He los - es for earth and for

heav - en   who los - es,   And   he wins for

ev - er   and   ev - er   who   wins.

No. 51.

MAESTOSO.

Great God, what-ev - er through thy

Church, Thou teach - est   to   be   true,   I

firm - ly   do   be - lieve   it   all,   And

shall   con fess   it   too.   Thou nev - er

cans't de - ceiv - ed   be,   Thou nev - er canst de -

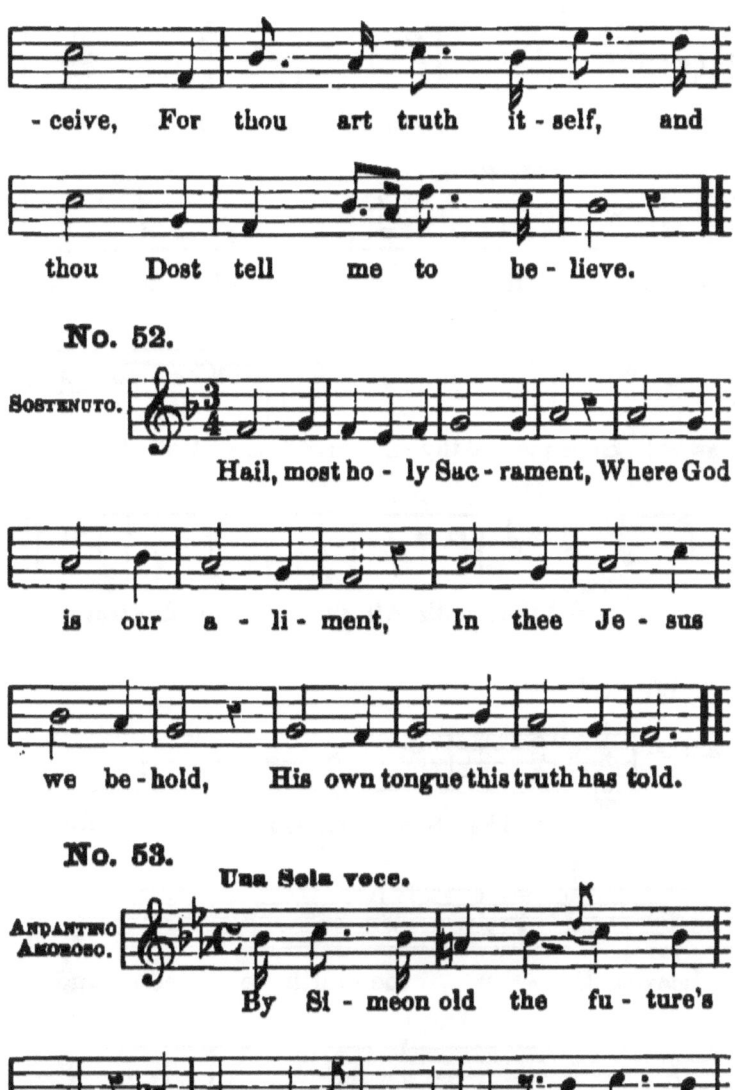

-ceive, For thou art truth it - self, and

thou Dost tell me to be - lieve.

No. 52.

SOSTENUTO.

Hail, most ho - ly Sac - rament, Where God

is our a - li - ment, In thee Je - sus

we be-hold, His own tongue this truth has told.

No. 53.

Una Sola voce.

ANDANTINO AMOROSO.

By Si - meon old the fu - ture's

told, Of God's In - car-nate Word, And Ma - ry's

15*

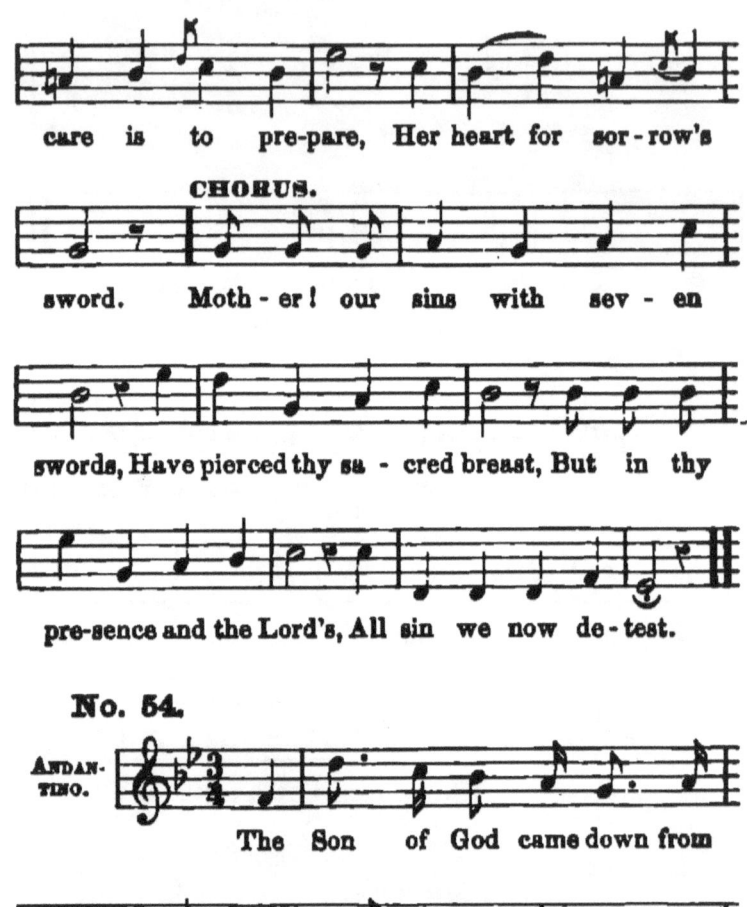

care is to pre-pare, Her heart for sor-row's

CHORUS.

sword. Moth-er! our sins with sev-en

swords, Have pierced thy sa - cred breast, But in thy

pre-sence and the Lord's, All sin we now de-test.

No. 54.

ANDAN-
TINO.

The Son of God came down from

heaven, Up - on the earth to dwell; And

man con-demns to cru - el death The

CHORUS.

heart that loved him well. Thou

go - est forth, O, bless - ed Lord, To

suf - fer death for me, And I, too, wish for

Lento.

thee to live, I wish to die for thee.

No. 55.

ANDANTE AFFETTUOSO.

An An - gel bent o - ver a

cra - dle, And seemed to be - hold mirrored

Piu Animate.

there, The light of his beau - ti - ful

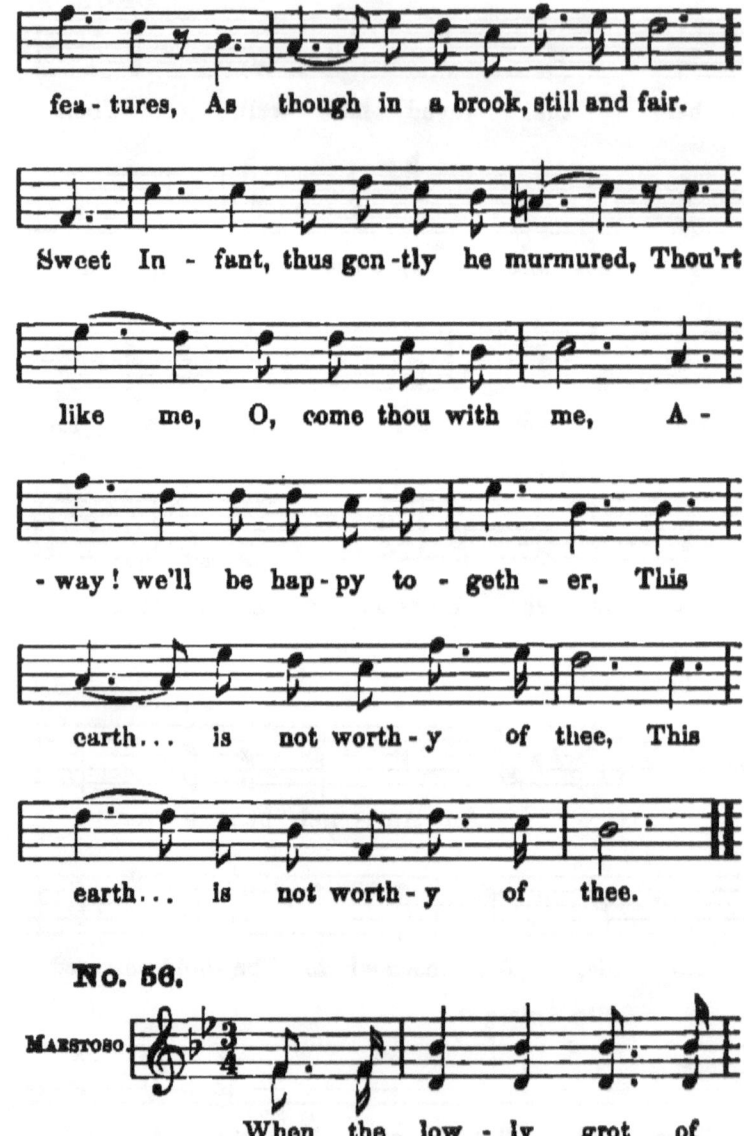

fea - tures, As though in a brook, still and fair.

Sweet In - fant, thus gen -tly he murmured, Thou'rt

like me, O, come thou with me, A -

- way ! we'll be hap-py to - geth - er, This

earth... is not worth - y of thee, This

earth... is not worth - y of thee.

No. 56.

MAESTOSO.

When the low - ly grot of

Bethlehem, First re-ceived the ho-ly child, On the

shep-herd's hum-ble offer-ing, The Re-

-deem-er kind-ly smiled. Faith and

Hope, and gen-tle Chari-ty, Those three

sis-ters, pure and fair, Were then

led by light from Heav-en, To ap-

-proach and wor- - -ship there.

No. 57.

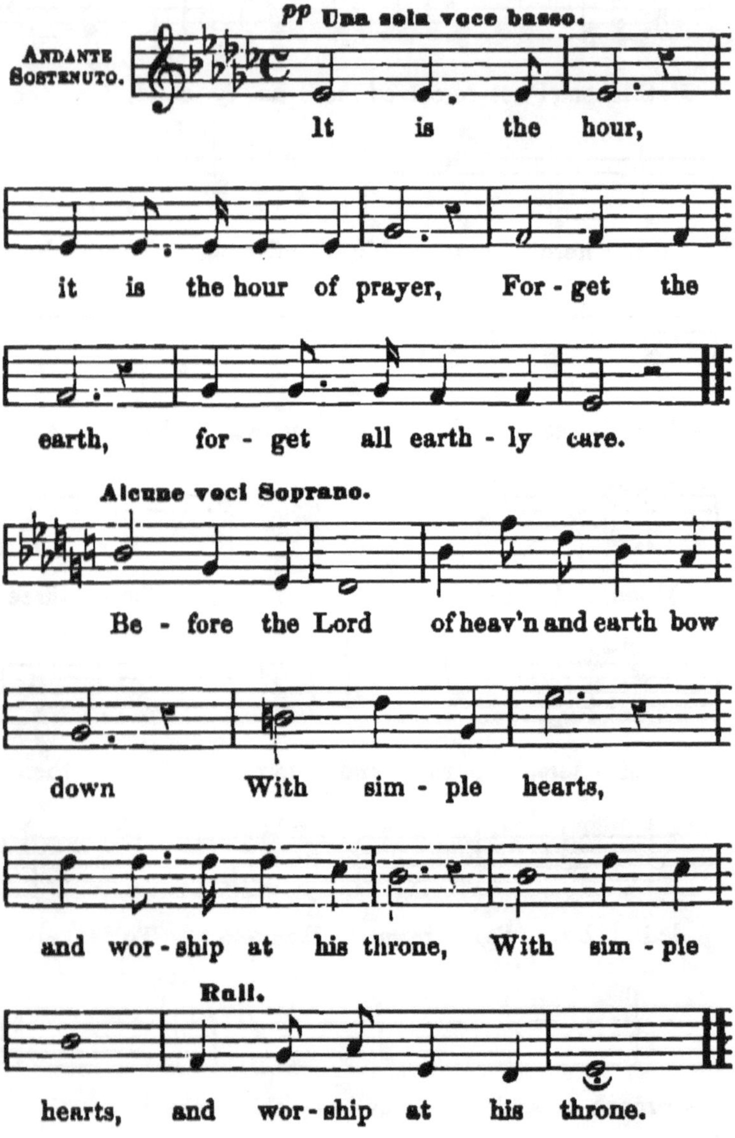

PP **Una sola voce basso.**

ANDANTE
SOSTENUTO.

It　　is　　the　　hour,

it　　is　　the hour　of prayer,　For - get　　the

earth,　　for - get　　all earth - ly　care.

Alcune voci Soprano.

Be - fore　the　Lord　of heav'n and earth bow

down　　With　sim - ple　hearts,

and wor - ship at　his throne,　With　sim - ple

Rall.

hearts,　and　wor - ship　at　his　throne.

CHORUS.

Fa - ther, Al-might - y, We are but dust,

In thy great mer - cy We put our trust.

Thou art our Mak - er, Thou art our Lord,

morendo.

By men and an - gels Thou art a - dored.

No. 58.

Affettuoso.

Queen of an - - gels

pray for, me, For my heart is

Full of thee. Thou art

next to God on high, First and

CHORUS.

fair - est, In the sky, First and

fair - est, In the sky.

No. 59.

Affettuoso.

Daugh-ter of God the Fa - ther,

O, Vir-gin pure and mild, I ve-ne-rate and

love thee, Ac - cept me for thy child.

My soul and all its pow - ers

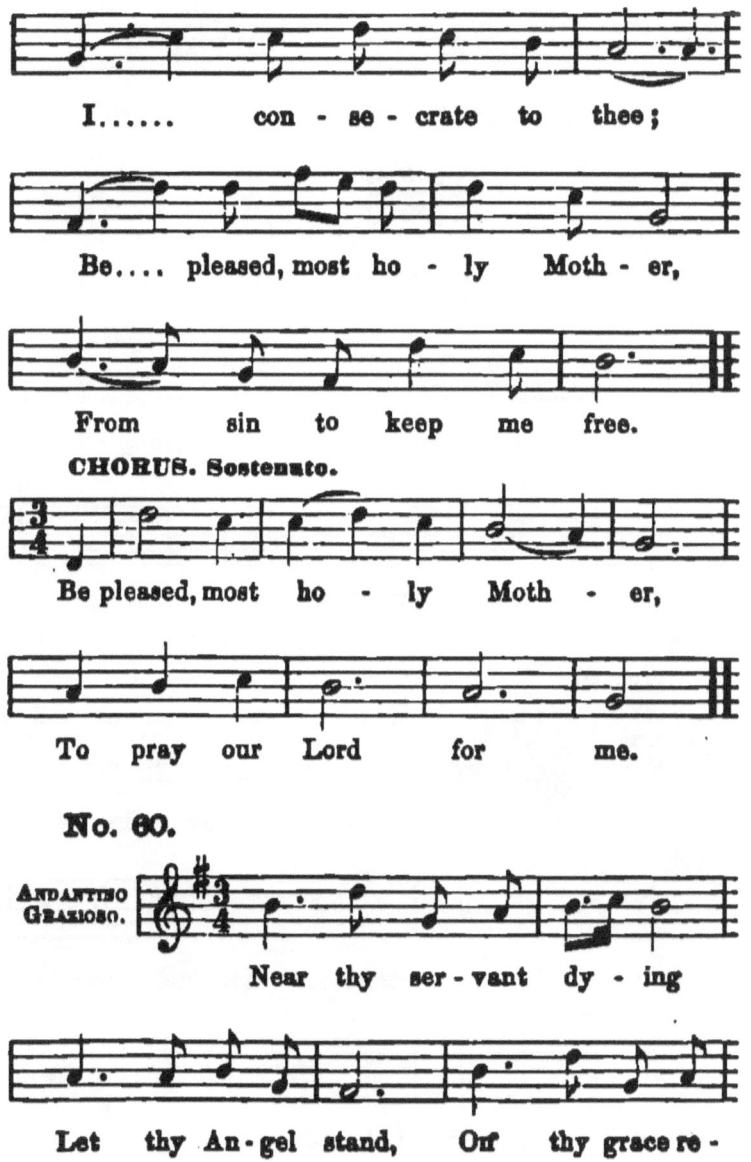

I...... con - se - crate to thee;

Be.... pleased, most ho - ly Moth - er,

From sin to keep me free.

CHORUS. Sostenuto.

Be pleased, most ho - ly Moth - er,

To pray our Lord for me.

No. 60.

ANDANTINO GRAZIOSO.

Near thy ser - vant dy - ing

Let thy An - gel stand, Or thy grace re -

- ly - ing, Let my heart ex - pand.

When these eyes no long - er See the light of

earth, Let my faith grow strong - er,

Shine with bright - er worth.

No. 61.

ANDANTE
SOSTENUTO.

Pun - ish me not in the

day of thy wrath, Strike me not sud - den - ly

down on my path; Let not the en - e - my

laugh at my fall, Pi - ty me, Lord, who hast

pi - ty for all. Judge of the fa - ther - less,

hope of the weak: Re - fuge and help of the

low - ly and meek, Look on my wretch-ed - ness,

list to my grief, Turn for thy mer - cy's sake,

grant me re - - lief.

No. 62.

Maestoso.

Yes, I have heard that whis - per,

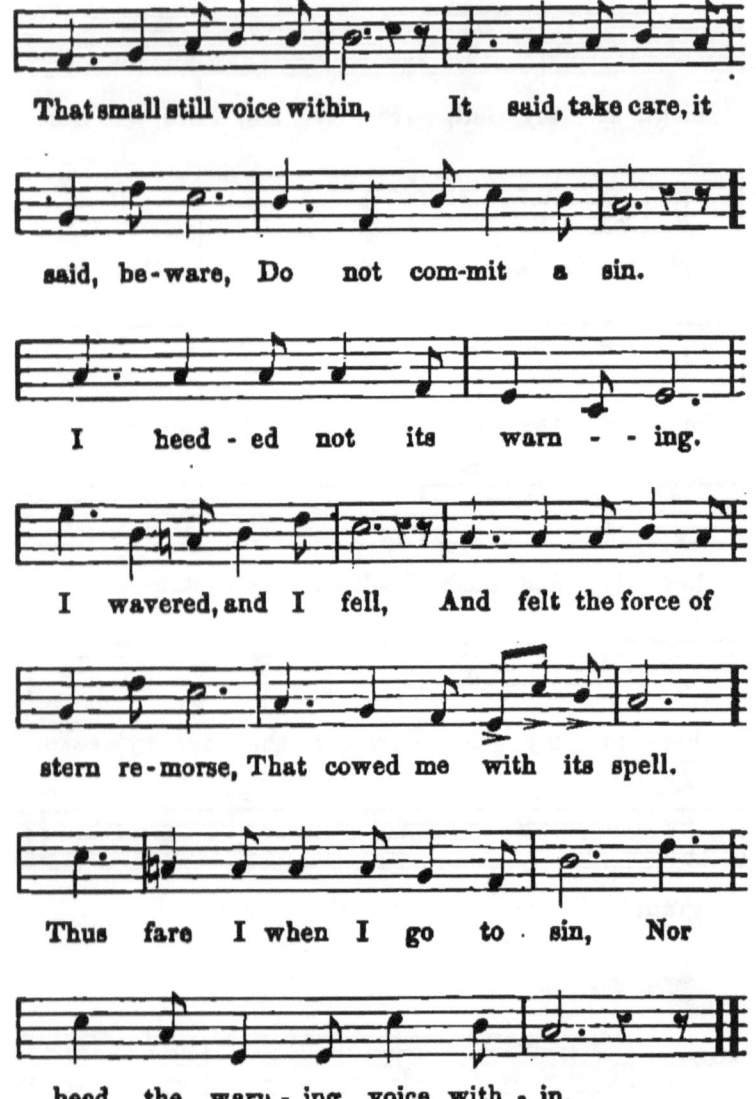

That small still voice within,   It   said, take care, it

said, be - ware, Do   not com-mit   a   sin.

I   heed - ed   not   its   warn - - ing.

I   wavered, and I   fell,   And   felt the force of

stern re - morse, That   cowed me   with   its   spell.

Thus   fare   I   when   I   go   to . sin,   Nor

heed   the   warn - ing   voice with - in.

CONTENTS.

CONTENTS.

CONTENTS OF AIDS TO MEMORY.

ALPHABETICAL INDEX.

ALPHABETICAL INDEX.

A indicates the page in " Aids to Memory."

CATALOGUE

OF

STANDARD CATHOLIC

AND

LITERARY WORKS,

Church Vestments, Altar Ornaments

AND

RELIGIOUS ARTICLES GENERALLY.

PUBLISHED, IMPORTED, AND FOR SALE

BY

P. O'SHEA, 104 BLEECKER
AND 183 GREENE-STREET.
1860.

P. O'SHEA'S
NEW PUBLICATIONS.

P. O'Shea, in submitting the following catalogue to the public, begs leave most respectfully to tender to the Catholic clergy and laity of America his thanks for their kind and flattering patronage. And he begs leave to assure to all his kind patrons, and to the Catholic community generally, not only a continuance on his part of the strictest attention to the orders of his customers, but he also engages, owing to increased facilities, to afford henceforward to the ARCHBISHOPS, BISHOPS, PRIESTS, RELIGIOUS COMMUNITIES, TEACHERS, and SUPERINTENDENTS OF EDUCATIONAL ESTABLISHMENTS, infinitely better opportunities of supplying themselves with every thing in the way of CHURCH VESTMENTS, ALTAR FURNITURE AND ORNAMENTS, and THEOLOGICAL, SCHOOL, and DEVOTIONAL BOOKS, than has ever hitherto been offered them in America. With this assurance he respectfully solicits not only a continuance, but an increase of the patronage of the Catholic community.

789 BROADWAY, NEW YORK, 1858.

The Silver Stole,

Being a collection of One Hundred Texts of Scripture, and One Hundred Original Epitaphs, suitable for the grave of a child.

BY REV. J. W. CUMMINGS, D. D.

1 vol., 8vo., cloth, gilt edges, $1.

"This is an extremely attractive volume, both in its getting up and in its contents. The epitaphs it contains are perfect little gems of poesy, and will serve many a loving mother as a means of giving expression to the feelings of her heart upon the loss of a dear child."—*Philadelphia Catholic Herald.*

"The Rev. J. W. Cummings, the eloquent pastor of St. Stephen's Church, has published a beautiful volume, for the benefit of the Ladies' Fair now being held at the Academy of Music, entitled 'The Silver Stole.' The work contains one hundred texts from Scripture, and one hundred epitaphs which they serve to illustrate, suitable for the grave of an infant. Apart from the beneficent object of this publication to promote the charities of the institution of the Sisters of Mercy, the work is one which reflects infinite credit upon the tastes and talents of the distinguished author."—*New York Illustrated News.*

"A very attractive and interesting volume has recently been published by the Rev. Dr. J. W. Cummings, for the benefit of the Ladies' Fair now being held at the Academy of Music, in behalf of the charities of the Sisters of Mercy. It is entitled 'The Silver Stole,' and contains a collection of one hundred texts of Scripture, and one hundred original epitaphs suitable for the graves of children. Independent of the charitable objects for which it is published, this little volume recommends itself to the heart of every parent who has lost a child, and who finds a religious consolation in that loss. It is a beautiful volume in its external and typographical appearance, and reflects great credit upon the liberality and ability of its accomplished author."
—*New York Daily News.*

Confraternity Manual;

OR,

-CATHOLIC GUILD-BOOK,

Being a Complete Manual of the Authorized Confraternities, Rosaries, and Indulgenced Devotions, compiled from approved sources, by REV. W. H. NELIGAN, LL. D.

1 vol., 24mo., Cloth			$0 37½
"	"	Roan, plain	0 50
"	"	" gilt	0 75
"	"	Turkey Morocco, extra	1 75

———

Legends of the Blessed Virgin Mary,

Translated from the French of

COLIN DE PLANCEY,

and published with the approbations of the Archbishop of Paris and of his Eminence Cardinal Wiseman.

1 vol., large 18mo., cloth, 50 cents.

———

Lingard's History of England.

New and complete edition, with the learned author's latest notes and revisions.

13 vols., 12mo. Illustrated with fourteen steel engravings.

Cloth	$10 00
Sheep, marble edges	13 00
Half Calf, marble edges	20 00

THE STAR OF BETHLEHEM.

A new and improved Manual of Prayer, compiled from approved sources by the Rev. Titus Joslin, with the approbation of the Most Rev. J. Hughes, D.D. 1 Vol. 810 pages, 18mo, printed on fine white paper.

Embossed roan, plain edges, one illustration .... $ 75
  "   " gilt " two " 1 25
American Morocco, gilt edges and sides...............1 50
  "   "   "   " clasps..................2 00
Turkey Morocco, extra 2 50
  "   " and clasps..........................3 0C
  "   " Bevelled edges 8 00
  "   "   " " and clasps...........8 5C
  "   " ornamented bands and clasps........4 50
Velvet, with ornaments, from $4 00 to $20 00.

What the Catholic Press say of it:

It compares favorably with any prayer book published in America.—*N. Y. Freeman's Journal.*

This manual reflects great credit on both the compiler and publisher. It contains over 800 pages of the best selected matter ever put into a prayer book, while the paper, printing and binding are in character with the contents.—*N. Y. Tablet.*

This is a prayer book of the largest class, but the cheapest in price, just issued. We observe that those litanies, which have been noticed by the most learned of our theologians, have been entirely omitted. This feature will certainly commend it, and we speak for it a liberal share of patronage.—*Baltimore Catholic Mirror.*

From our own experience, we can say there is hardly any work so hard to find as a PRAYER BOOK, containing the various devotional aids which a Christian requires in daily life. The STAR OF BETHLEHEM is most satisfactory in this respect. All the principal services of the church, all the ordinary necessities of the Christian are copiously provided for. The prayers at mass, as well as the preparation for confession and communion, are especially full. *The Vespers also form a noteworthy feature of this volume. It includes the proper psalms for every feast in the year, accompanied by its appropriate bar of music, placed neatly and conspicuously over the psalms.* In short, the STAR OF BETHLEHEM is a prayer book that can be relied upon. It is printed beautifully, carefully, and attractively—is illustrated with well executed and appropriate steel engravings, and is substantially bound in a variety of styles to suit the means of every Catholic.—*N. Y. Truth Teller.*

This very excellent compilation includes the gospels and

epistles for the year, and various offices, special devotions, and masses, in addition to the usual contents. The book is well printed in large clean type, and will be found a useful companion and guide to the holy temple.—*Philadelphia Catholic Herald.*

We observe throughout this manual many useful notes and remarks, proofs of the Rev. Father Joslin's zeal for the interest and welfare of the people entrusted to his care.—*Baltimore Metropolitan Magazine.*

Just Published!

THE PARADISE

OF

THE CHRISTIAN SOUL,

DELIGHTFUL FOR ITS CHOICEST PLEASURES OF PIETY OF EVERY KIND.

BY

JAMES MERLO HORSTIUS,

OF THE CHURCH OF THE BLESSED VIRGIN MARY IN PASCULO PASTORIS AT COLOGNE.

A NEW AND COMPLETE TRANSLATION,

By Lawful Authority.

The Paradise to the Christian Soul, to which access hitherto was only had in the Latin language, is the most complete manual of Catholic devotion, meditation and instruction, ever published. It contains nearly 1100 pages of closely but beautifully printed matter, remarkable for its sweet and fervid piety, and its choice and useful instruction. It is beyond all other books a Family Prayer Book, and a copy of it should be in every Catholic family.

TERMS.

Roan, plain embossed.............1 steel engraving $1 25
"   gilt   " 2   "   "   1 50
Am'n Morocco, gilt edges and sides 4   "   "   1 75
Turkey Morocco, extra............6   "   "   8 00
Turkey Morocco, extra and clasps..6   "   "   8 75
Turkey Morocco, bevelled edges....6   "   "   8 50
Turkey Mo'co, bev'ed edges, clasps.6   "   "   4 25
Turkey Mo'co, bands and ornam'ts.6   "   "   5 50

☞ Any of the above styles will be sent by mail, prepaid, on receipt of the annexed retail price.

What the Catholic clergy generally say of the Paradise of the Soul:

"IT IS THE GREATEST WORK OF PRAYER, MEDITATION AND IN-STRUCTION, EVER OFFERED TO THE CATHOLIC PUBLIC."

What the Catholic press say of it:

It contains the most soul-elevating prayers we have ever read.—*Philadelphia Catholic Herald.*

The principal feature of this book is that it combines the best characteristics of a prayer and meditation book. We have often seen whole libraries which did not contain so much truth and beauty.—*N. Y. Tablet.*

HISTORY
OF THE
PONTIFICATE AND CAPTIVITY
OF
POPE PIUS VI:
TOGETHER WITH A GLANCE AT THE CATHOLIC CHURCH.

TRANSLATED FROM THE FRENCH BY MISS H***TH, A GRAD-UATE OF ST. JOSEPH'S, NEAR EMMITSBURG, MD.

1 VOL. 18MO CLOTH, 240 PP. 50 CTS.

A more intensely interesting narrative has rarely, if ever, been written. The heroic devotion and constancy of the Pope, the insanely rabid conduct of his persecutors, his meekness under every contumely, *their* vexation at the calm resignation with which he bore every affront, together with the many important events which then agitated the Chris-tian world, invest this volume with an interest which rarely attaches to any book.

The Young Communicants.

BY THE AUTHOR OF "GERALDINE."

1 VOL. 18mo, CLOTH, 25 CTS.

It is unnecessary to point out the merits of a book written by the Author of GERALDINE. It may not, however, be out of place to say that FATHER JOSLIN especially recommends it as a most instructive and interesting book, in a note in that excellent prayer book, the STAR OF BETHLEHEM.

The Sufferings of Jesus,

BY

CATHERINE EMMERICH.

TRANSLATED BY A SISTER OF MERCY.

1 VOL. 18MO, CLOTH, WITH A FINE STEEL ENGRAVING OF THE "AGONY IN THE GARDEN," 37 1-2 CTS.

NOTICES OF THE PRESS.

This is a very attractive little volume, relating to the passion and death of our Saviour. The authoress is represented as having been favored with visions during the holy season of Lent, in which she spiritually witnessed the progress of the "Sufferings of Jesus." What was thus revealed to her she describes in a graceful style, which this condensed translation presents unimpaired to edify the reader.—*N. Y. Truth Teller.*

Persons of contemplating minds can have no better guide to the thrilling scenes of calvary than the Sufferings.—*N. Y. Tablet.*

Here is an excellent book, and is a valuable addition to our books of devotion. It is got out in good style, and is embellished with a beautiful engraving of our blessed Lord in his agony.—*Boston Pilot.*

THE STAR OF THE NORTH.

Life of the Right Rev. Bishop Maginn.

BY

THOMAS D'ARCY McGEE, ESQ.

1 VOL. 12MO, CLOTH, 75 CTS.

NOTICES OF THE PRESS.

The Life of this great champion of the Irish church, so full of apostolic zeal, moral courage and iron fortitude, cannot fail to attract the Catholic reader.—*Baltimore Catholic Mirror.*

The history of the RIGHT REV. BISHOP MAGINN is the history of one of the most deeply interesting epochs of Irish history—the close of a religious struggle for the freedom of religious worship, and the beginning of a yet unfinished struggle for national independence * * *. We commend this book as a valuable addition to Irish literature in America, which Mr. McGee has done so much to foster, and to establish.—*Philadelphia Catholic Herald and Visitor.*

We have not often read so interesting a work as this memoir is.—*N. Y. Truth Teller.*

A MONTH OF MAY;

OR SCENES FROM THE

Life of the Blessed Virgin Mary.

ARRANGED FOR THE DEVOTIONS OF THE MONTH OF MAY, WITH PRACTICES, PRAYERS, AND EXAMPLES.

1 VOL. 32MO, CLOTH, 25 CTS.

SOME OF THE NOTICES OF THE PRESS.

This is a precious little jewel case, containing a number of the most precious pearls of the crown of the Immaculate Virgin Mother. They are really brilliant, quite free from common-place, and wrought in sparkling style, so that they are beyond all praise. We warmly commend this beautiful book to every household. It cannot be read without having our love for our Blessed Lady increased.—*Philadelphia Catholic Herald.*

This little book is a gem. * * * It is beautifully gotten up.—*N. Y Freemen's Journal.*

LIFE
OF
ST. FRANCIS OF ASSISIUM.
BY
REV. TITUS JOSLIN.

1 VOL. 18MO, CLOTH, GILT BACKS, 87 1-2 CTS.

NOTICES OF THE PRESS.

Thank you, FATHER JOSLIN, for writing this interesting and earnest little volume.—*N. Y. Freemen's Journal.*

It is a charming history of the life of one of the humblest and most devoted servants of the Lord.—*N. Y. Truth Teller.*

Bickerton; or the Immigrant's Daughter:
A TALE OF THE TIMES.

BY THE AUTHOR OF "HARRY LAYDEN," &c.

1. VOL. 12MO, CLOTH, 50 CTS.

NOTICES OF THE PRESS.

This is an excellent story and well suited to the times.—*Brownson's Review.*

Any work like the Immigrant's Daughter, whose tendency is to wither or uproot bigotry and intolerance, ought to be welcomed by every man who loves the country and its institutions, and is animated by the holy principle of Patrick Henry—"Give me liberty or give me death."—*N. Y. Citizen.*
BICKERTON; OR THE IMMIGRANT'S DAUGHTER. *P. O. Shea,* Publisher, 739 Broadway.

This is an excellent little work of fiction, grounded on the present aspect of political affairs in this country. It is a true narrative of the sufferings of many a poor immigrant, and will be read with interest.—*N. Y. Irish American.*

This is an interesting story, and will be read with great interest at the present time, as it dips into the Know Nothings in grand style. The book is well gotten up by the publisher.—*Boston Pilot.*

THE
CATHOLIC
USEFUL AND ENTERTAINING
LIBRARY.

COMPOSED OF BIOGRAPHIES, TALES, AND OTHER
WORKS OF AN AMUSING AND INTERESTING
CHARACTER, TRANSLATED AND ORIGINAL.

This library has been projected to remedy a want long
felt in the Catholic literature of the United States, namely,
that of a collection of edifying narratives and tales, combin-
ing amusement and instruction, not above the capacity of
the young, nor beneath the attention of the old, and furnish-
ing a substitute for the pernicious novels and other light
works of which the press is so prolific. The first, second,
third and sixth numbers have been supplied by the distinguished Redemptorist, Father Hewit. Father Bresciani,
the author of the "Life of the Egyptian Aloysius,"* a translation of which forms numbers two and three of the series,
has already acquired a world-wide reputation as the author
of the "Jew of Verona." Regarding the other volumes of
the series, the publisher guarantees that they shall be worthy associates of those already named. Besides the best of
lighter biographies and tales, translated from foreign lan-
guages, the publisher will endeavor to intersperse original
works of a similar kind, by American Catholic writers.

In order, however, that he may be able to secure the co-
operation of our best writers in this undertaking, a large
share of patronage from the Catholic public will be necessary. He, therefore, respectfully solicits the reverend Clergy,
and all others interested in the circulation of a wholesome
Catholic Literature, to lend their countenance and influence
to his enterprise. That it may be within the means of all to
supply themselves with this valuable library, the price of
each volume, printed on fine paper, and neatly bound in
muslin, will be only 37 1-2 cents.

* Abulcher Disclarah is called the "Egyptian Aloysius."

L

𝕷𝖎𝖋𝖊 𝖔𝖋 𝕲𝖚𝖊𝖓𝖉𝖆𝖑𝖎𝖓𝖊,

PRINCESS BORGHESE.

TRANSLATED FROM THE GERMAN, WITH AN INTRO-
DUCTION BY THE REV. A. F. HEWIT, PRIEST
OF THE CONGREGATION OF THE
MOST HOLY REDEEMER.

We are delighted to see this admirable little Life of so
exemplary a Catholic of our own times. The subject is one
of interest, and the style of the translator is particularly
agreeable.—*N. Y. Freeman's Journal.*

We have often to commend books with words of praise,
since no other would be exactly suitable, although they
scarcely merit what the words convey. The present volume
is an exception. It is in reality equally interesting and
edifying, and forms a most promising commencement of
the New Catholic Library commenced by Mr. O'Shea. The
Life of Guendaline Talbot reads like a story of romance, yet
it is all true."—*St. Louis Leader.*

◆◆◆

𝕮𝖆𝖙𝖍𝖔𝖑𝖎𝖈 𝖀𝖘𝖊𝖋𝖚𝖑 𝖆𝖓𝖉 𝕰𝖓𝖙𝖊𝖗𝖙𝖆𝖎𝖓𝖎𝖓𝖌 𝕷𝖎𝖇𝖗𝖆𝖗𝖞, 𝕹𝖔𝖘. 2 & 3.

LIFE OF

THE EGYPTIAN ALOYSIUS;

OR

𝕿𝖍𝖊 𝕷𝖎𝖙𝖙𝖑𝖊 𝕬𝖓𝖌𝖊𝖑 𝖔𝖋 𝖙𝖍𝖊 𝕮𝖔𝖕𝖙𝖘.

BY

REV. FATHER BRESCIANI.

TRANSLATED FROM THE ITALIAN BY REV. A. F. HEWIT,

C. S. S. R.

2 VOLS. CLOTH, PER VOL. 87 1-2.

NOTICES OF THE PRESS.

This is one of the most delightful little biographies we have ever laid eyes on, and we hope it will find its way into every Separate School, and every other Catholic institution in the Province. A life of a Saint of the ancient Coptic Church is a rarety, especially such an extended one as the present. There are two volumes, the one containing 147 pages, and the other 120. It is published by Mr. P. O'Shea, Broadway, New York.—*Toronto, Canada, Mirror.*

This English version is beautiful and facinating. It is put forth as a literal one; but while we doubt not that it is an exact reproduction of the original, we can recognize in it none of the dryness or stiffness of style characteristic of proclaimed literal translations. Indeed, we cannot see any noble feature in the English dress of the memoir, that is not to be discerned in the translator's edyfying introduction. The artistic and glowing touches of the same evenly guided pen are visible throughout the whole work, and one must be hypocritical to an extreme who fails to observe and appreciate the many charming merits either of the original prefatory remarks of the translator, or the translation of the biography itself.

Had we room, we would gladly quote some portions of the work, which seemed to us singularly beautiful and entertaining. However, we are obliged to content ourselves with what we have said in favor of the publication, and again recommending it to the notice of every thoughtful Catholic reader.—*N. Y. Truth Teller*

CATHOLIC USEFUL AND ENTERTAINING LIBRARY, NOS. 4 AND 5.

EDMA AND MARGUERITE;

A Tale.

BY THE AUTHOR OF THE "ORPHAN OF MOSCOW."

2 VOLS. 18MO, CLOTH, GILT BACKS, PER. VOL. 87 1-2. CTS

NOTICES OF THE PRESS.

It is a highly pleasing story for young persons, illustrative of the duty, pleasure and reward of filial devotion, charity, and friendship.—*Philadelphia, C. Herald.*

A truly edifying and interesting story.—*N. Y. Truth Teller.*

LIFE
OF A
MODERN MARTYR,
(BISHOP BORIE.)
By Rev. A. F. Hewit.
1 VOL. 18MO, CLOTH, GILT BACKS, 37 1-2 CTS.

NOTICES OF THE PRESS.

This is another of Father Hewit's edifying little books. His name is a sufficient recommendation, yet we cannot avoid calling especial attention to this life of a faithful servant of God, not alone on account of the Christian heroism it illustrates, and the attractive style in which it is presented, but also because the subject of Catholic missions is one which deserves the greatest attention.—*N. Y. Freeman's Journal.*

This beautiful book presents to us a memoir of one of the most truly heroic men of modern times. His burning zeal led him to the remote regions of Tonquin to spread the conquests of Christianity, where he labored, in despite of the most cruel persecution, until his blood was shed under the glorious banner of the cross.—*Catholic Herald.*

THE BEST MEDITATION BOOK.
Just Published—
CRASSET'S MEDITATIONS
For every Day in the Year.

TRANSLATED FROM THE FRENCH BY MRS. ANNA H. DORSEY, WITH AN INTRODUCTION BY REV. C. WALWORTH.

1 Vol. Large 12mo, Cloth, 620 pp. Price $1.50.

The Rev. Father WALWORTH, in his Introduction, says:— "Of Meditation Books we know of none which seem to fulfil their purpose, except this work of FATHER CRASSET. . . . . . . We repeat once more for those who aspire, not simply to read Meditations, but to practise Mental Prayer, this work of FATHER CRASSET is the book of books."

Notices of the Press on Crasset's Meditations.

These Meditations, perhaps the most popular and celebrated of any in Europe, rich in matter and well-arranged

P. O'SHEA'S

CATALOGUE

OF

CHURCH VESTMENTS,

ALTAR FURNITURE

STATUES,

STATIONS OF THF CROSS,

Paintings for Churches,

Religious Engravings, plain & color'd,

Rosaries, Crucifixes, Medals, &c.

Missals, Breviaries, Ceremonials,

AND

Religious Articles generally.

New-York:

P. O'SHEA, 104 BLEECKER

AND 163 GREENE-STREET.

1860.

I.

VESTMENTS.

Vestments per set, viz.: chasuble, stole, maniple, chalice
   veil, pall and burse—of cotten velvet.. $ 12 00 to 16 00
   "   "   "   " ornamented cross 14 00 to 18 00
   "   "   "   " damask "   " 16 00 to 24 00
   "   "   "   " superfine damask,
   "   " and richly embroidered cross 35 00 to 60 00
   "   "   "   " of silk, plain, and
very neat.......................... 25 00 to 40 00
   "   "   "   " superfine heavy,
silk, with embroidered or gold cross,
flowers, etc., fine galloons, and fringes 50 00 to 100 00
   "   "   "   " silk velvet, richly
embroidered, gold galloons and fringes, 60 00 to 120 00
   "   "   "   " gold cloth, *demi fine* 40 00 to 70 00
   "   "   "   "   "   " very fine 100 00 to 150 00

MISSION VESTMENTS—ALL COLORS.

Silk galoons, easily folded, etc.,................$16 00 28 00
  SETS OF DALMATIGUES, to suit the above, supplied at about
20 per cent. less than double the price of set of vestments
indicated above.
Copes—cotton velvet...................... $24 00 to 30 00
  " damask, or light silk, with flowers
      and some embroidery............. 35 00 to 50 00
  " fine silk, or silk damask, interwoven
      with fine gold and flowers, or em-
      broided with gold and chenile......70 00 to 120 00
  " imitation, gold cloth...............35 00 to 45 00
  " fine, "   " ....80 00 to 150 00
Benediction veils, various styles............12 00 to 50 00
Baptismal stoles, "   " .... 2 00 to 6 00
Preaching stoles, "   " .... 5 00 to 50 00
Albs of fine linen, trimmed with lace....... 8 00 to 25 00
Surplices, plain or trimmed with fine lace... 4 00 to 16 00
Altar lace, plain, per yard................. 31 to 2 50
  " " interwoven with gold, per yard.. 3 50 to 6 00
Cinctures of different kinds................. 75 to 3 50
  " for Bishops....................... 8 75 to 15 00
Priest's caps, of cloth or velvet............ 2 75 to 5 00

II.

ALTAR FURNITURE.

Chalices, plated for missions, 8 to 9 inches,
with leather cases.................. $10 50 to 14 00
" with't   "   " .... 9 00 to 12 50
" with silver cup, and silver patina, from
8 to 9 inches, with case............ 16 00 to 24 00
" silver cup and patina, 10 inches...... 26 00 to 35 00
"   "   "   "   "   " heavily }
gilt .. } 34 00 to 48 00
"   "   "   "   " 11 inches " 30 00 to 40 00
"   "   "   "   " " heavily }
gilt } 42 00 to 52 00
"   "   "   "   " 12 inches " 33 00 to 45 00
"   "   "   "   " " heavily }
gilt } 45 00 to 60 00
" All solid silver, 10 inches, finely fin'ed......... 45 00
"   "   " 10 " and gilt.. 55 00
"   "   " 11 " finely finished 60 00
"   "   " 11 " very heavily gilt...... 80 00
"   "   " 11 " gothic, ornamented,...110 00
Ciboriums to match the above at prices about 5 per cents
less.
Chappelles—containing chalice and ciborium, 10
inches high, with silver cups, cru-
ets of glass encased in richly gilt
bands, and small altar bell, all
richly gilt...................... $120 00
" containing the same, but of a little
larger size 140 00
" solid silver, from............ 180 00 to 240 00
Ostensoriums, gilt rays, 16 inches................ 14 00
"   "   " 18 " 16 00
"   "   " 20 " 21 00
"   "   " 22 " 27 50
"   "   " 22 " set with stones.... 34 00
"   "   " 24 " 40 00
"   "   " 26 " 48 00
"   "   " 26 " set with stones.... 56 00
"   "   " 28 " 50 00
" all gilt, 28 " 60 00
" solid silver 24 " 120 00
" with very rich ornaments set with
stones, all heavily gilt, and finely chased, 30 inches, ... 120 00
Gongs, different sizes, from................ 12 00 to 24 00

● Chimes, and Altar bells, various sizes.
Sanctuary lamps, silver plated, 8 inches in diam.... 12 00
  " " " " 10 " " 15 00
  " " " " 12 " " 22 00
  " " " " 12 " "
            richly ornamented 85 00
 "   "   " gothic style, from. 30 00 to 60 00
Censors, silver plated, small size.................... 7 50
  " " " medium " 10 00
  " " " " " ornam'ted......... 12 00
  " " " large size, and " 16 00
  " all gilt, and finely chased................. 24 00
A naviculum, silver plated or gilt, to correspond with
     the censor, accompanies it.
Holy water pots, with asperges, silver plated,
          small size 7 50
  " " " " " medium " 9 00
  " " " " " large size 12 50
  " " " " " all gilt " " 22 50
Crosiers, imported to order.
●Procession crosses, highly polished, brass... 8 00 to 20 00
  "   " silver plated........... 10 00 to 25 00
●Oil stocks, solid silver...................... 5 00 to 12 00
Pyxes " " .... 4 00 to 12 00
 "   " gold .... 15 00 to 25 00
Altar cards, small size, illuminated border,
    and handsomely gilt frames per set.... 8 75
 " " medium size, illuminated, gothic
     borders, fine gilt frames.............. 6 00
 " " large size, splendidly illuminated,
    and richly framed, from...... 8 00 to 15 00
Bread irons, with cutters, all well made, per set...... 10 00
  " " to make two, three, and five
     breads, with cutters, from 18 00 to 80 00
Stations of the cross, finely painted on canvass,
     30 by 40 inches, unframed 140 00
  " " " same style, in gilt frames.... 220 00
  " " " consisting of fine lithographs,
     varnish'd and stretch'd up-
     on canvass, and looking as
     well as an oil painting, 26
     by 36 inches, richly framed 110 00
  " " color'd lith's, neatly fram'd, at
     all prices, according to the
     size of picture, and style of
     framing, from ... 10 00 to 100 00
● Candelabra, per pair, from............... 12 00 to 40 00
● Brass candlesticks, Paris style, finely finished,
  14 inches, per pair .... 5 00 .

16	inches,	per pair	....	6	00
18	"	do.	....	7	50
20	"	do.	....	8	50
22	"	do.	....	10	50
24	"	do.	from...............12 00 to 16	00	
26	"	do.	" .... 14 00 to 18	00	
28	"	do.	" .... 16 00 to 20	00	
80	"	do.	" .... 18 50 to 24	00	
82	"	do.	" .... 21 50 to 27	50	
84	"	do.	" .... 25 00 to 31	00	
•86	"	do.	 28	00	
88	"	do.	 82	00	
42	"	do.	 86	00	

Crucifixes, well and carefully finished, and made to match the different sizes of candlesticks, can be had for the same price as a corresponding pair of candlesticks.

Crucifixes of bronze, silver, and ivory, always on hand in great variety.

☞ Clergymen, or others, ordering church vestments, or altar furniture, and not having an opportunity of examining them, can, if the articles should not be found suitable, return them, or exchange them, within a reasonable time from the date of delivery.

Candles, wax, of a superior quality, per lb............65 cts.
    "   sperm, from,............ "   85 cts. to 50 "
Incense,...................... "   75 "

Paschal candles, made to order, and sent to any part of the United States, Canadas, etc., etc.

Statues, of all sizes and styles, on hand, or imported to order, at short notice.

III.

RELIGIOUS ARTICLES.

BLACK ROSARIES.

No. 1.	Black,	on brass chain,	per doz.	.... $		25
" 2.	do.	do.	do.	....		40
" 8.	do.	do.	do.	....		50
" 4.	do.	do.	do.	....		70
" 5.	do.	do.	do.	....	1	00
" 6.	do.	do.	do.	....	1	25
" 7.	do.	brass bound crucifix,	per doz.	....	2	20
" 8.	do.	on steel chain,	do.	....	1	80
" 9.	do.	do.	do.	....	2	40
" 10.	do.	do.	do.	....	8	00
" 1.	Red,	on silver plated chain,	do.	....	1	20
" 2.	do.	do.	do.	do.	....	1	50

No. 8.	Red,	on silver plated chain, per doz					1 75
" 4.	do.	do.	do.	do.	....		2 10
" 5.	do.	do.	do.	do.	....		2 75
" 1.	White,	do.	do.	do.	....		1 30
" 2.	do.	do.	do	do.	....		1 56
" 8.	do.	do.	do.	do.	....		1 75
" 4.	do.	do.	do.	do.	....		2 25
" 5.	do,	do.	do.	do.	....		8 00
" 6.	do.	do.	do.	do.	....		8 75
" 1.	Black silver chain and crucifix,			do.	....		8 50
" 2.	do.	do.	do.	do.	....		10 50
" 8.	do.	do.	do.	do.	....		13 50
" 4.	do.	do.	do.	do.	....		18 00
" 5.	do.	do.	do.	do.	....		80 00
" 1.	White, imitation ivory, do.			do.	....		7 75
" 2.	do.	do.	do.	do.	....		9 00
" 8	do.	do.	do.	do.	....		12 00
" 4.	do.	do.	do.	do.	....		18 00
" 5.	do.	do.	do.	do.	....		24 00
" 6.	do.	do.	do.	do.	....		80 00

Red at the same price as the white.

ROSARIES.

Cornelian, agate, ivory, pearl, and garnet, strung on silver, on silver gilt, and on gold, always on hand, at moderate prices.

CASES FOR ROSARY BEADS.

Cases, in the form of eggs, apples, pears, etc., to contain rosaries of different sizes, are always on hand, from, per doz. 75 cents and upwards.

BRASS-BOUND CRUCIFIXES.

No. 1.	Brass-bound crucifixes,	2½ inches, per doz...				$ 1 50
" 2.	"	"	3½	"	"	.. 2 20
" 8.	"	"	4	"	"	.. 2 75
" 5.	"	"	4½	"	"	.. 8 75
" 6.	"	"	5½	"	"	.. 5 00
" 7.	"	"	5½	"	"	.. 6 00

Large sizes, different prices, according to the elegance and workmanship with which they have been executed.

CRUCIFIXES ON STANDS.

No. 1. Brass figure, on imitation ebony cross, 6 inches, per doz.................................... $ 90

No.	2.	Brass figure	on small Eb. cross, 9¼ inches..	1 25

No. 2. Brass figure on small Eb. cross, 9¼ inches.. 1 25
" 3. do. do. do. 10 do. ... 1 50
" 4. do. do. do. 11 do. ... 1 75
" 5. do. do. do. 12 do. ... 2 25
" 6. do. do. do· 14 do. ... 3 25
" 7. do. do. do. 16 do. ... 5 00
" 8. do. do. do. 18 do. ... 8 00
" 9. do. do. do. 20 do. ...10 00
" 10. do. do. do. 21 do. ...12 00
" 11. do. do. do. 22 do. ...15 00
" 12. do. do. do. 24 do. ...18 00

Brass, silver plated, gilt and ivory crucifixes on stands at various prices.

GOLD AND SILVER MEDALS.

No. 1. Gold medal of the Immaculate conception.... $ 75
" 2. do. do. do. 1 00
" 3. do. do. do. 1 50
" 4. do. do. do. 2 75
" 5. do. do do. 3 75
" 1. Silver medal do. do. 04
" 2. do. do. do. 06
" 3, do. do. do. 10
" 4. do. do. do. 15
" 5. do. do. do. 25
" 6. do, do. do. 38
" 7. do. do. do. 56
" 8. do. do. do. 1 00
" 9. do. do. do. 1 50
" 10. do. do. do. 2 75

Gold and silver medals of the Redeemer, St. Joseph, St. Patrick, St. Aloysius, St. Bridget, St. Philomena, the Angel Guardian, etc., etc., constantly on hand.

BRASS AND PLATED MEDALS.

No. 1. Per gross...................................$ 45
" 2. do. 59
" 3. do. 70
" 4. do. 90
" 5. do. 1 20
" 6. do. 2 00
" 7. do. 3 40
" 8. do. 5 00
" 9. do. 6 75
" 10. do. 9 60

These include medals of the IMMACULATE CONCEPTION,
SEVEN DOLORS, SACRED HEART, St. Joseph, St. Patrick, Confirmation and Communion medals, etc., etc.

SCAPULARS AND SCAPULAR PRINTS IN GREAT VARIETY.

SACRED PRINTS.

*Several on a sheet, steel engraving, and used for illustrating
prayer books. Size of the sheet, W. 19, H. 13.*

	Per hundred. Plain.	Colored.
ONE HUNDRED AND EIGHTY different plates, 4, 6, 8, 10, 12, 16, 18, 20, 21, 24, 25, 32, 40, 50, etc., on the sheet; Saints, Crucifixion, Virgins, Emblems..................... $4 62		$7 75
The same, with gilt border 7 75		15 50
The same, on colored glazed paper 15 50		
The same, on colored glazed paper, and with gilt border............................18 75		
TWENTY-EIGHT different plates, 8, 10, 12, 16, 21, 32, on the sheet; Saints, Virgins, etc.... 6 25		
The same, with gilt border.................. 9 50		25 00
The same, on colored glazed paper..........15 50		
The same, on colored glazed paper, and with gilt border............................18 75		
THIRTY-FIVE different plates, 16 on the sheet— Life of our Lord, Holy History, etc., etc.. 7 75		31 00
The same, with gilt border..................12 50		38 75
The same, on colored glazed paper..........18 75		
The same, on colored glazed paper, and with gilt border............................21 75		
THIRTY different plates, of 12, 16, and 32 on the sheet; Saints, Virgins, Angels, emblems, 9 25		29 00
The same, with ornamented borders.........23 00		

LACE PICTURES.

Engraved prints, with a lace edge representing virgins,
saints, crucifixions, etc., etc., and used as book marks.

As this class of pictures contains over 2000 different
patterns, it is almost impossible to give a descrip-
tion of each kind. They may be ordered by stating
the amount required, and a good selection will be sent.
The sizes are, for books, 72mo. 48mo. 32mo, 18mo. They
are made plain, colored, gilt edge, on rice paper, embossed, illuminated with small brilliant stars, folding
with fancy envelopes, different shapes, etc., etc., etc.;
prices from 7 cents up to $30 00 per dozen.

COMMUNION AND CONFIRMATION TICKETS.

	Per hundred.	
	Plain.	Colored.

Two SHEETS with 2 drawings on each—Communion for boys and girls, No. 705; confirmation for boys and girls, No. 706.....4 75   10 00

THREE SHEETS with 4 drawings on each—Communion, No. 713; confirmation, No. 714;
communion, confirmation, and baptism,
No. 715 ....4 75   10 00

VARIOUS RELIGIOUS SUBJECTS.

	Plain.	Colored.

THE LAST SUPPER. Fine lithograph from Leon-
ard de Vinci. W. 28, H. 19.............. 0 98   1 86

THE ASSUMPTION OF THE BLESSED VIRGIN. From
the Titian. W. 18, H. 28................ 0 98   1 86

THE TREE OF LIFE, (engraved,) representing
the history of the Church. W. 21, H. 30, 0 62   2 17

THE IMMACULATE CONCEPTION. By C. Mez. W.
14, H. 19 .... 0 62   1 55
The same on India paper.................. 1 00
This is the most perfect copy of the celebrated
painting by Murillo, bought from Marshal Soult
for the Louvre.

JESUS IN THE GARDEN OF OLIVES. Very fine
mezzotint, by Tony. W. 27, H. 21....... 1 86   4 65

ELEVEN LARGE LITHOGRAPHS by Tassaert, etc.
19 by 26................................ 0 40   0 80

1. Jesus Washing the feet of the Apostles.
2. Jesus Preaching in the Temple.
3. Jesus Entering into Jerusalem.
4. Miraculous Draught of Fishes.
5. Jesus Restoring to life the Son of the Widow of Naim.
6. Jesus Blessing the Children.
7. Sacred Heart of Jesus.
8. Sacred Heart of Mary.
9. Patriarch St. Joseph.
10. St. Anthony of Padua.
11. Our Lady of Mount Carmel.

The same ones on dark ground 3 00

	Plain.	Colored.

TWENTY-EIGHT RELIGIOUS SUBJECTS, W. 15, H. 20 0 40   0 80

1. Adoration of the Wise Men.
2. Jesus in the Garden of Olives.
3. Jesus Driving the Buyers and Sellers out of the
   Temple.

4. Jesus Restoring to Life the Daughter of Jairus.
5. Jesus Salvator Mundi, (crucifixion.)
6. Jesus taken down from the Cross.
7. The Visitation.
8. The Samaritan Woman.
9. St. Joseph.
10. St. Vincent of Paul.
11. The Immaculate Conception.
12. St. Frs. Xaveria.
13. Jesus Walking on the Waters.
14. The Holy Family.
15. The Guardian Angel.
16. St. Francis of Sales.
17. Jesus carrying his Cross.
18. Communion of St. Jerome.
19. The Crucifixion, (from Van Dyck.)
20. Jesus carrying his Cross, (Rubens.)
21. The Annunciation, (Coypel,) mezzotint.
22. The Flight into Egypt, (from Coypel,) mezzotint.
23. The Resurrection, mezzotint.
24. Ecce Homo, (bust.)
25. Mater Dolorosa, (bust.)
26. St. John, (bust.)
27. St. Mary Magdelen, (bust.)
28. Virgin Mary, (the good Mother.)

A large variety of plain and colored Lithographs besides those mentioned above always on hand, at prices varying from $3 00 to $20 00 per hundred.

MEDALLIONS.

36 different kinds of Medallions: Silver with Glass over and Gold Border, Head of the Saviour, with Oval Frame, Ecce Homo, Mater Dolorosa, and several other Drawings, with Black or Brass Oval Frames, Convex Glass, Nos. 1801 to 1836....................... $8 76 to 119 44 per doz.

HOLY WATER FONTS.

117 different kinds of Holy Water Fonts, Brass Figures, Ivory, Silver, Carved Ivory, Ivory Gothic Frame, with Velvet Ground, Bronze, Nos. 1901 to 2017...... $1 03 to 110 16 per doz.

BOOK MARKS.

Book Marks : Silk Ribbon, Brass,
Silver, Ivory Crosses, etc., Nos.
2101 to 2104 .... $2 82 to   4 90 per doz.

STATUES.

150 different sizes Biscuit Statues of
the Blessed Virgin, St. Joseph,
Angels, Holy Water Fonts, &c..... $0 03 to $9 72 each.
47 of the above patterns, richly gilt
and ornamented .... 0 22 to 11 34   "
20 different Statues, Ivory and Silver,
on fine Carved Ivory Stand .... 0 41 to 13 26   "